Introduction

Over the past two decades, the proliferation of personal computers has overwhelmed marketers with tools intended to make their jobs easier and more productive. Marketing has moved into the scientific realm with statistics, demographics, complex spreadsheets, forecasting models, checklists, and processes. Intuition, creativity, and innovation have been lost amid endless meetings and countless hours spent populating reports and spreadsheets.

I don't want to diminish the importance or value of these tools, but I believe marketing is more than demographics, statistics, and processes. I'm convinced that in any successful marketing campaign there is still a place for a more intuitive approach—maybe even a metaphysical approach—to defining and positioning products and identifying new markets. In this book, you won't find the 5 Ps of marketing, SWOT or TOWS analyses, or forecasting techniques. I avoid what I think are boring formalities and memorizations. Instead, I guide you through a story set in ancient China in which the Taoist sage, Lao Tzu and *The Art of War* author, Sun Tzu, use their combined wisdom to explain how to use the chaos of the market to help find customers, identify market segments, and define successful products.

The book begins…well, at the beginning. That may sound strange, but people tend to prefer starting at the end of a story, where the answers are hidden and ignore the beginning, where the questions are. How will you find an answer if you don't know the question? Lao Tzu forces his student, Hong-meng, to start at the beginning where the question is and then follow the path through the chaos to find the answer. He teaches him that success begins with the first step, telling him, "*The voyage of a thousand leagues begins with the first step.*"

According to Lao Tzu, a market is not defined by statistics and demographics but is a *"form without form. The image without image. It is fleeting and elusive."* It is chaos.

Lao Tzu and Sun Tzu demonstrate that finding a product's competitive advantage is not a process of simply checking off a list of features. Features describe the product; you must look beyond the features to define its real value. According to Lao Tzu *"one fashions the clay to make a vase, but it's the emptiness inside that makes it useful."* Customers are also more than a statistic or an entry in a forecast. They are complex, dynamic, and multidimensional. *"The more one speaks of it the less one can hold it."* When you look in a mirror, you only see a reflection of reality. If you don't understand your customer, then just like what you see in the mirror, you'll never see the real customer, but only his or her reflection.

According to the Tao, the world came from chaos. It was the Tao that brought form and direction. Lao Tzu explains that *"the Tao is fleeting and unholdable—it presents an image that is fleeting and unholdable, it is however something."* The market is like the Tao—it also begins in chaos: "It is however something." It needs intuition and a creative and innovative marketing plan to bring form, direction, and, ultimately, success.

Throughout the text the quotes of wisdom from Lao Tzu and Sun Tzu are shown in *italics*. A list of references can also be found at the end of the book.

THE MARKET IS CHAOS

The Tao of Marketing

STEVE BURNS

ISBN: 1470013266

ISBN 13:   9781470013264

Library of Congress Control Number: 2012902224
CreateSpace, North Charleston, SC

By imagination and reason we turn experience into foresight;
we become the creators of our future,
and cease to be the slaves of our past.

—*Will Durant, The Story of Philosophy*

contents

1

THE QUESTION

> The voyage of a thousand leagues begins with the first step.
>
> —Lao Tzu

The Zhou dynasty
China, 500 BC

Nothing. There was nothing as far as he could see. Kunlun Mountain was the highest peak in the area, and he should've been able to see something - but there was only an endless view of nothing. Leaning against a boulder, he stared into the distance, searching for anything buried in this unending nothingness. He sighed and waited patiently. He didn't know exactly what he was waiting for, but he wasn't going to leave until he found it.

Kunlun was a magical mountain. It was home to the eight immortals of Tao and was thought to be the source of answers to impossible questions. Hong-meng had come to the magical mountain in search of answers. How long had he been staring into the distant nothingness? He didn't know. Time didn't exist on the magical mountain, but he felt as though he'd been sitting there forever.

He remembered the look on his wife's face when he'd told her of his plans. She didn't understand his need for answers. She'd never understood. But his daughter did—or, at least, she pretended to. She was young enough to believe that her father always knew what he was doing. Hong-meng's son was just the opposite. He was at the age where he had all the answers.

Hong-meng had left early the next morning. His wife stood in front of their house, crying quietly, swearing that he was deserting his family. His daughter waved happily as he walked slowly down the path, and then, seeing her mother cry, decided to cry too. He glimpsed his son peeking out from behind the door, pretending he didn't care if his father left or not.

The journey to Kunlun Mountain had been long and hard. He'd been tired and very lonely. Every morning he'd awoken with doubt clawing at his stomach. Was he doing the right thing? Would he find the answers he sought? He was certain only that he couldn't quit.

He had chosen a spot on the summit above everything, a spot from which he could see to forever and beyond—but forever seemed to be full of nothing. Nothing! He was beginning to hate that word! Tie Gai hadn't warned him about the nothingness.

Tie Gai was probably his best friend, although Hong-meng never knew when he was being serious or just telling a story. Tie Gai had arrived in Qufu, the capital city of Lu Province in the southern region of the Zhou Empire, several years ago. Hong-meng remembered the first time he saw him. It was an early summer morning, and Tie Gai was walking through the small alleyway leading from the open market just outside the walls of the inner city. He nodded at Hong-meng and smiled in greeting as he passed and then, without asking permission, set up his stall next to Hong-meng's small shop. Tie Gai was a miracle worker with wood. He could make anything you wanted. He loved to talk and had an opinion about everything, although he never discussed himself or where he came from. The two men spent hours together, talking about every subject imaginable—or, more accurately, Tie Gai talked while Hong-meng listened.

It was during one of these one-sided conversations that he'd told Hong-meng about Kunlun Mountain. He claimed it was a magical place where one could find answers to anything. No question was too difficult. Hong-meng suspected that this was Tie Gai's way of trying to help solve Hong-men's problems.

That same night, Hong-meng decided he must go to Kunlun Mountain. He needed answers.

But Tie Gai hadn't told him about the nothingness!

Hong-meng took a deep breath, trying to relax, and looked for a more comfortable place to sit on the rocky ground. He stared harder into the endless nothingness. It didn't help. Frustrated, he stared even harder, until his eyes began to hurt. He knew that in nothing there was always something. It was impossible for nothing to exist without something. It was like yin and yang—one couldn't exist without the other. Would he really find what he was looking for? He stared intently, trying to rip apart the nothingness. He knew something was buried in there. He just had to find it.

Finally, out of the colorless nothing, a form began to appear! Hong-meng stared harder, rubbing his eyes and trying to focus on it. It looked like a long stick. A walking stick! He blinked to see if the image would disappear. Was it only his imagination, or was there really a walking stick moving through the nothingness? The image didn't disappear. He now saw a hand attached to the walking stick, and attached to the hand was an arm. The walking stick was pulling the arm through the nothingness up to the summit of Kunlun Mountain. As it neared, he could make out the crooked body of an old man attached to the arm.

The old man was wearing a long wool cloak and a large straw hat that completely hid his face. He seemed to float through the nothingness, moving effortlessly up the slope and finally settling on a spot directly opposite Hong-meng. He crossed his legs and laid his walking stick on the ground, slowly removing his straw hat to reveal his face. It was round and held together by wrinkles, with dark eyes that glowed with amusement. A thin wisp of beard hung from the centre of his chin, and shoulder-length gray hair framed his face, giving him a strange, almost crazy look.

"Hello, Hong-meng," the old man said calmly. Hong-meng couldn't tell if the man was smiling or if the wrinkles just made it look like a smile. Not sure how to respond, he bowed deeply at the waist, waiting for the old man to continue. The wrinkles moved again as the old man bowed in return and said, "My name is Li Er Dan."

Hong-meng studied the man closely. He thought he recognized the name. He knew it from somewhere, but where? He dug into his memory for the answer. In the recesses of his mind, he could see Tie Gai kneeling in front of his worktable carving a small wooden figure. While he worked, he told a story of someone he'd met in the past, but Hong-meng was only half listening. Eventually

Tie Gai held up the figure in the light, admiring his work. Hong-meng looked at the small wooden object—a man with a walking stick and a broad hat. He couldn't help but ask, "Who's that?"

"His real name is Li Er Dan," replied Tie Gai. "But today, everyone calls him…"

"Lao Tzu?" Hong-meng said aloud, not sure if he was making a statement or asking a question. He couldn't believe it! He was sitting at the top of Kunlun Mountain talking with the master of Taoism! Hong-meng smiled.

"Yes, that's what people call me," the old man replied, smiling and bowing his head. "I was on the island of Beng Lai with Han Xiang Zi and Cao Guo Jin, two Tao immortals. We were having an interesting discussion on the meaning of progress and how it needs to be built on innovation and creativity when I received the message that you wanted to see me."

Hong-meng was surprised—and confused. He hadn't sent any message. He'd only come to Kunlun Mountain because he didn't know where else to find help.

"Yes, I know," replied Lao Tzu, understanding the confusion. "I heard your thoughts. That's how I knew you wanted to talk to me."

Hong-meng nodded, feigning agreement, although he was unsure of what to make of the wrinkled old man. He felt intimidated sitting opposite someone as important as Lao Tzu. The rocky ground began to feel even more uncomfortable and he couldn't find a spot for his hands. Silence stretched on until he couldn't stand it anymore. He had to fill it with something. "I'm looking for answers," Hong-meng said nervously, taking a chance that he was allowed to speak.

Lao Tzu smiled, as if humoring a small child, and replied gently, "Of course you are. Everyone is."

"Can you help me find them?" Hong-meng asked quietly, hoping he wasn't being too forward.

"No," Lao Tzu answered simply.

"Huh." Hong-meng was taken aback. He couldn't think of anything else to say, so he just sat with his mouth open, staring at the old man.

"Huh," Lao Tzu repeated, then laughed. "'Huh' isn't a word, it's just a sound," he said. "Instead of 'huh,' I think you meant to ask why I can't help, didn't you? Why did I say no—isn't that what you really want to know?"

Hong-meng nodded slowly. He decided it was easier to agree than say something else.

Lao Tzu laughed again, enjoying Hong-meng's confusion, and then explained, "No, I can't help you find the answers. First we have to find the questions."

"Huh," Hong-meng said again, becoming even more confused.

The wrinkles on Lao Tzu's face deepened into a frown. "Huh," he repeated again. His voice held a note of impatience as he added, "Instead of 'huh,' you should be asking me to explain what I mean."

Hong-meng tried to hide his confusion, "What do you mean?"

"That's better," Lao Tzu replied, and the wrinkles changed direction to form a laugh.

Hong-meng felt his face grow warm, adding embarrassment to his confusion. He waited for the old man to continue, deciding that it was probably safer to remain silent.

"You're trying to start at the end," Lao Tzu stated in a more serious tone. He paused to see if Hong-meng had anything to say, but seeing that he hadn't understood the importance of the statement, he continued, "Everybody wants to start at the end." Again he paused, but this time more for effect than in expectation of response. "It seems to me that people always have the answers before they even know what the questions are." He shook his head as if he didn't understand why people couldn't see what was obvious. "But you can't do that. You must start at the beginning, where the questions are. Then you can follow the path to the answers." Lao Tzu finished the statement in a quieter, more reflective voice, staring across the nothingness as if looking for the beginning of a path that would lead to the answers. Hong-meng stared into the nothingness alongside him, also searching for the beginning of the path, but he couldn't see anything—only nothingness.

Still shaking his head, Lao Tzu continued, "Finding the question isn't easy. *He who claims it is easy, rarely holds his word.*" He sounded as if he were talking to himself and had forgotten about Hong-meng. After a brief pause, as if he had just noticed Hong-meng, he began to chuckle. "At least, it's not easy to find the right question. You must understand that questions aren't always what you think they are. They camouflage themselves and hide behind other questions that aren't really relevant. If you don't find the right question, then you'll follow the wrong path and never find the right answer. That makes it more difficult. Do you understand?" he asked, although Hong-meng knew Lao Tzu didn't really expect an answer. "You need to know what question you're looking for. It's too easy to grab the first one that comes to mind." He emphasized the point by reaching upward to grab at an imaginary question. "Make sure you find the right one." He looked down at his empty hand.

He glanced at Hong-meng to make sure he was listening. Lao Tzu saw that he was, but knew Hong-meng hadn't really understood what he was saying. Hong-meng was still waiting to find answers without looking for the question. *Everybody seems to ignore the obvious*, he thought to himself sadly. For some strange reason, people always tried to hide the obvious in something more complicated. They wanted things to be complex. Why? Maybe because they were scared of the obvious. It's safer to stay hidden in the complicated. Or maybe they were just embarrassed because they hadn't thought of it themselves. It was clear that Hong-meng refused to see the obvious. He wanted to ignore the beginning and start at the end.

Lao Tzu had seen many instances where people refused to see the obvious. They always tried to bury it in a dark maze of complexity so that they could ignore it.

Tao was a good example. Lao Tzu had always taught that Tao was life. It was as simple as that. For Tao, there was no beginning or no end, since they were both the same. Tao was everywhere and nowhere because everywhere and nowhere were the same thing. One couldn't exist without the other. That was obvious, Lao Tzu thought. Or at least it should've been obvious, just as the question was the beginning and the answer was the end. He also knew that people could be taught the obvious. It wasn't impossible; it just took time.

Lao Tzu thought back several years to one of his visits to the province of Wei. He'd arrived in a small farming village one evening, where the local shaman received him as an honored guest. During dinner he learned that as in most small villages, the residents' lives were governed by the *wou* and the *hi*—the witches and the sorcerers. The villagers had heard of Tao from the *wou* and *hi,* but the way it had been explained to them made it sound too complicated for their simple lives. Their existence was driven by the four seasons and the benevolence of the *t'ien*—the heavens. The shaman explained that the people saw their destinies in readings from the sacred bones and didn't need the complexities of Tao.

Lao Tzu listened to what the shaman was telling him, but even more importantly he heard what he was saying. Hidden behind the words was the truth: the *wou* and *hi* felt threatened by anything out of their direct control or influence. And they felt threatened by Tao. They had buried the simplicity of Tao under layers of complexity to protect themselves. He knew the *wou* and *hi* were the beginning, and the beginning was where the problem was. Since he knew where the beginning was, all he had to do was follow the path to the solution. Lao Tzu spent a week in the village visiting with the *hi* and *wou*, explaining the simplicity of Tao so they could see that it wasn't a threat to their influence. He explained that Tao was everything and nothing—it was existence and nonexistence, the combination of yin and yang. One could not exist without the other. It was so big that it had no exterior, and it was so small that it had no interior. He explained that *the Tao is to the universe as the river beds and valleys are to the river as it travels to the sea.* It did not threaten their magic; in fact, since Tao was everything, it was obvious that the magic of the *wou* and *hi* was Tao. It took a week of gentle persuasion, but the *wou* and *hi* finally began to see the obvious. Their magic was part of Tao. Tao and their magic were the same thing.

Life was simple when you could see the obvious. "Life doesn't need to be complicated," Lao Tzu told Hong-meng, smiling. "If you don't know where the beginning is, you'll never find the end. You can't have an end without a beginning. You can't have an answer without a question."

Lao Tzu took a deep breath and fell silent, lost in his own thoughts. Hong-meng tried to hide his impatience as he waited for the old man to continue. Finally Lao Tzu said, "When you've found the right question, it's time to follow the path to where the answer is." Hong-meng nodded slowly, hoping Lao Tzu couldn't sense his irritation. He hoped the path to the answers wasn't too long. The ground had become unbearably uncomfortable and he was beginning to wish he could go home. He followed Lao Tzu's gaze into the distant nothingness, wondering where the beginning of the path was.

"It's not an easy path to follow. It twists, it turns, and it has dead ends." Lao Tzu's voice grew stronger and more confident to emphasize the importance of what he was saying. "Rushing blindly forward is a mistake. Patience will show you the correct path. If you have patience, *the most difficult thing in the world will reduce itself to the most basic elements.* Every question has an answer, and it's not that difficult to find if you have the right question and the patience to follow the right path—one step at a time." He paused briefly before adding, "*The largest task will be accomplished in small steps.*"

Hong-meng was still nodding, but it wasn't a confident nod. He wasn't sure what all this had to do with him. The beginning, the end, the small steps—it all seemed like nonsense to him. He just wanted to find his answers and go home.

"It's not easy," Lao Tzu continued.

"Finding the answers isn't easy?" Hong-meng asked, trying to make it sound more like a statement than a question. He already knew that finding the answers wasn't easy, he thought with rising frustration. That's why he'd come to Kunlun Mountain in the first place!

"No," replied Lao Tzu, shaking his head in frustration. It was clear that Hong-meng hadn't understood anything he'd said. "Finding the answer is easy—" he emphasized the point by slapping his hand on his knee "—but to have an answer without a question is just an opinion. It's not an answer. First you have to find the right question." Hong-meng was nodding again. It had become an automatic reflex. Lao Tzu smiled and continued, "To do that, you have to admit that you don't know what the question is. Only then will you look for it. *To know that it's not known is excellence. Not to know that it should be known is an error.* I've met too many people who use ignorance to hide from questions. They don't like questions that will make their life difficult because difficult questions may give them answers they don't want to hear. Instead they prefer to invent answers they like so they never have to look for the question."

Lao Tzu paused to make sure Hong-meng was listening, then turned to gaze into the distant nothingness again as if there were something there only he could see. In a quieter voice, almost as if he were talking to himself, he said, "*The voyage of a thousand leagues begins with the first step.*" He glanced back to Hong-meng and repeated the last three words. "The first step—it begins with the first step. It's not easy, and sometimes the path is very long and sometimes you bump into other questions along the way. You're likely to get lost if you don't stay focused on the real question."

"The question is the first step. The real question," Hong-meng repeated, sounding more confident than he felt. He stared at the old man, blinking to make sure he was awake. Maybe this was only a dream. It wasn't exactly what he had expected to find at the summit of the magical mountain.

Lao Tzu grew serious. "Unfortunately, finding the right question and following the right path isn't always enough." He paused. "Remember you said that the first step was the real question." Hong-meng nodded. "You were right, but that's not all. The first step of the voyage is very important, but there is more to the first step than just the real question."

"More?" Hong-meng wondered if he would ever be able to go home.

Lao Tzu nodded. "First, you must *want* to find the answers. That probably sounds strange, but you'd be surprised how many people say they're looking for answers but don't really want to find them. Second, you have to *believe* you can find the answer. Without wanting and believing, you're wasting your time." Anger sounded in his voice as he continued, "There are people who will never be able to do it. Do you remember when I told you that there are people who hide in ignorance so that they never have to look for the question? Well, there are also people who do just the opposite. They spend all their time finding new questions so they never have to find the answers. Why? Because they're afraid of answers," he said with disdain. "They hate answers. They only want more questions. They treat problems the same way. They're always looking for more problems because they're afraid of solutions. When they get close to a solution, they panic and start looking for more problems." He stopped and took a deep breath, trying to push his anger aside.

He shifted his position so that he could look directly at Hong-meng. "Maybe you're different? It seems to me that you might have the right attitude," he said calmly, his frustration now under control.

Hong-meng wasn't sure how to respond. To avoid making a mistake and embarrassing himself, he lowered his eyes and waited for Lao Tzu to continue.

"You're not like these other people," Lao Tzu said. "You aren't afraid of questions because you aren't afraid of finding the answers. You came here because you want to find the answers. You wouldn't have suffered through the long voyage if you didn't believe you could find them."

That made Hong-meng feel better, but he still didn't believe he was any closer to finding the answers. Lao Tzu was looking at him without saying anything, which made him uncomfortable. The silence began to bother him enough that he felt he had to fill it with something. "Does that mean I can find my answers?"

Lao Tzu frowned.

"I mean, can I find the questions?" he corrected quickly. "Am I smart enough to find the questions? You said it isn't easy. Can I learn how? Can you teach me?"

2

THE PROBLEM

> **Intelligence isn't learning. Learning isn't intelligence.**
>
> —Lao Tzu

"Can I teach you?" Lao Tzu laughed at Hong-meng's question. He quickly recognized the desperation in Hong-meng's voice so he changed to a more serious tone. His eyes became more intense and focused as he looked directly at Hong-meng and asked, "Are you smart enough? Tell me, what do you mean by being smart enough? Is that the same as being intelligent?"

Hong-meng thought for a moment and then nodded, but it wasn't a confident nod.

"I agree," Lao Tzu said. "At least, in today's world, being smart is just another way of saying someone is intelligent. But what is intelligence?" He paused. *"Intelligence isn't learning. Learning isn't intelligence."*

Hong-meng nodded again, not sure he understood.

Lao Tzu's voice seemed to grow sad. "At my age, I've seen too many people who consider themselves intelligent but don't really know how to learn. They think they're very intelligent—and maybe they are. Being intelligent can be a strength, but it can also be a weakness."

"A weakness?" Hong-meng asked, confusion apparent in his voice. He had always felt intimidated by people he thought were more intelligent than him. He didn't understand how being intelligent could be a weakness. It should make people stronger, shouldn't it?

"Yes, a weakness," Lao Tzu replied. "For some reason we measure intelligence by the amount of knowledge someone has." He could see that Hong-meng agreed. "But *intelligence isn't learning*, and *learning isn't intelligence*. These are simple truths that everybody ignores. Measuring intelligence by how much you have learned can be misleading. Learning creates knowledge—that's true. But just collecting knowledge is not the same as real intelligence." He could see that he now had Hong-meng's complete attention. "In my experience, I've always seen the same three major weaknesses in intelligent people.

"The first is that they don't understand that knowledge itself can be the biggest obstacle to finding new knowledge. Knowledge is a difficult barrier to cross. It's always easier to have enough knowledge and not need any more. Intelligent people think their knowledge is the end, and not just the beginning. When they have enough, they stop looking for new knowledge. For them, knowledge becomes a huge barrier," Lao Tzu explained.

Now this Hong-meng understood, in part because he'd seen it many times—especially during his early days as a student. His father had had plans and ambitions for his son that went well beyond being a simple craftsman. He saw his son becoming a *shi*, an administrator in the local Lu government, but that required training—and knowledge. Hong-meng was sent to classes taught by the local master, where he could learn the rituals and laws that were an essential part of government. He endured months of rigorous training, painfully memorizing and rehearsing countless rituals. He quickly learned that memorization was the key to success. Questions that went beyond existing knowledge were not allowed; they were seen as a threat.

"Yes, it's dangerous not to allow questions to be part of knowledge," Lao Tzu said, as if reading Hong-meng's thoughts. "If you accept that knowledge must include questions, then it becomes a tool to finding more knowledge. Memorization on its own becomes the end and not the beginning." He smiled. "The question is the beginning and the answer is the end, but if the answer creates more questions, then that is the beginning of true knowledge. Knowledge should be like the Tao. It should have no beginning and no end.

"The second major weakness is that people don't see knowledge as a tool. They see it as something static. They collect knowledge and store it away. A tool only has value if it is used to create something else. Intelligent people are measured by how much knowledge they have stored away, not by how well they use that knowledge."

Hong-meng agreed. As a student he had been measured by how well he could repeat his lessons. He was never taught how to use the knowledge he was given.

Lao Tzu smiled at the realization that Hong-meng understood what he was saying. He continued with his lecture. "Intelligent people also have another problem—the third major weakness," he stated. "They're afraid to make mistakes. They need to be perfect, and perfect people don't make mistakes. Being afraid of making mistakes can be even worse. People need to understand that making mistakes can be an advantage. *He who is conscious of his error will no longer commit the error.* Making mistakes is what breaks down the barriers of old knowledge so that we can find new knowledge. That's real intelligence."

Lao Tzu sighed deeply and continued, "Maybe you are smart enough. You know now that the answers aren't what you're looking for. It's the questions you need to find—the first step of the voyage. You won't let intelligence and knowledge get in the way of learning." He reached across and laid a hand on Hong-meng's shoulder. "Even more important, you've already shown you know how to listen, and if you know how to listen, you'll be able to learn."

"Listen and learn?" repeated Hong-meng unconsciously. He was trying to convince himself that he really understood what Lao Tzu was saying.

"That's good! If you listen, you'll learn. That's the secret to finding your questions—and your answers."

Suddenly the wind began to pick up across the summit of Kunlun Mountain. Lao Tzu listened to the sound. Hong-meng imagined he could hear a voice saying, "*Don't listen with your ears, listen with your mind.*"

Lao Tzu looked annoyed. "Thank you for your wisdom, Zhuang Zhou." Looking back to Hong-meng, he asked, "Do you know Zhuang Zhou? No, of course not! He's a Taoist monk. Or at least he will be. He hasn't even been born yet, but since time doesn't exist here, he's able to interfere in things that don't concern him." The wind died down and the sound of laughter followed it as it disappeared into the nothingness.

Lao Tzu tapped his fingers impatiently against his knee and waited for the wind to completely disappear. His body began to relax and his hands stilled. "Zhuang Zhou was right," he admitted reluctantly. "It's an important lesson to remember. The mind and the mouth can't normally work at the same time. And to make it even worse, too many people make a direct connection between their ears and their mouth, without using their mind to filter the information. Listen and learn. Use your ears as a doorway into your mind. Use your mind as a source of information for your mouth. Speak only when you have something to say. You don't need to be afraid of silence. Don't talk just to make noise to fill the empty silence. To *speak rarely is to conform to nature.*"

"Speaking rarely will help me find the questions?" Hong-meng asked, trying to get back to solving his own problem but not understanding how he could ask questions without speaking.

"Of course it will," replied Lao Tzu, surprised at the question. "You came here to find answers. Now you know you really came here to find the right question. Do you know what that question is?"

Hong-meng looked depressed. "No, I'm not sure I know yet," he replied. "I know what my problem is, but I'm not sure what the real question is. What question will give me the answers to solve my problem?" He paused, thinking about what he'd already learned, and then said confidently, "You said I needed to start from the beginning. Maybe the problem is the beginning."

Lao Tzu nodded, his dark eyes glowing with satisfaction. "And if you understand what the real problem is, you can probably find the right questions to ask. If you take the whole problem and tear it into smaller, manageable pieces, you'll probably find the right question hidden there somewhere. *Perceive the smallest; that is clairvoyance.*"

Hong-meng had heard that statement before. Tie Gai had said the same thing. He was always accusing him of being too serious and making problems bigger than they really were. Instead, Tie Gai had said, he should look for the smaller problems in the bigger problem. His lectures were always amusing, but Hong-meng never understood how he could make his problems into small problems. Problems were just problems—and they were always big problems.

Lao Tzu sat quietly in the silence of Hong-meng's thoughts. After a respectful pause, he made himself more comfortable on the rocky ground. "Let's look at your problem and see if we can find the real question hidden there."

What was the problem? thought Hong-meng. He saw the old man watching him with his wrinkled smile and calm eyes, surrounded by the nothingness at the top of Kunlun Mountain. *Why did I come here?* he asked himself for the hundredth, maybe the thousandth, time. How long had it taken him to travel from Qufu to the magic mountain? Weeks? Perhaps months? He didn't know. Time didn't seem to exist anymore. His wool cloak was dirty and ragged with holes at the elbows and frayed cuffs. His hair was long and scraggily, and he'd long ago given up trying to keep it tied in a knot at the top of his head. His moustache was tangled in his chest-length beard. He looked down at the cloth bag that was beside him and caressed it with his fingers, as if that might help solve his problem.

"The problem is…" he began, and then stopped, not knowing what else to say.

"The problem is…" repeated Lao Tzu, encouraging him to continue.

"The problem is that nobody wants my product," Hong-meng said finally, the words spilling out in an embarrassed haste. "Nobody wants my product," he said again, this time with sadness, as if it were a personal insult. He slowly untied the cord around the cloth bag and pulled out the metal tip of a plough. He handed it to Lao Tzu, who took it from him and laid it on the ground without comment. Next, Hong-meng pulled out a knife made from the same metal and handed it to Lao Tzu.

"Is this your problem?" Lao Tzu asked, placing the knife on the ground next to the plough tip.

Hong-meng shrugged and quietly said with pride, "Iron. My tools are made of a new metal called iron. They're much better than the bronze tools that everybody uses now." He pulled out another tool, the head of a small hand ax, and passed it to Lao Tzu. "My tools are stronger, sharper, and last longer than any bronze tools." He looked out into the nothingness surrounding the magical mountain of Kunlun and added, "But nobody wants them. That's my problem."

"That's your problem," Lao Tzu repeated, shaking his head. "And you couldn't find anybody to help you solve your problem?" He picked up the knife and inspected it more closely.

"No. I couldn't find anybody. Some people just listened and nodded but didn't say anything. Some actually told me I didn't know what my problem was," Hong-meng said angrily. "Others told me to talk to the sorcerer for help. What does a sorcerer know about iron tools?" He shook his head in frustration. "I'd either get a look of understanding but no answers, or totally ridiculous suggestions that had nothing to do with my problem."

Lao Tzu smiled. *"Those who know, don't speak. Those who speak, don't know."*

"So how can I find someone who knows and who will speak?" Hong-meng asked impatiently. "My workshop is full of iron tools that nobody wants. Can you help me?"

"Your problem is like the nothingness," Lao Tzu replied, gesturing to the wide expanse beyond Kunlun Mountain. "*Seems to be very profound, appears to last forever.*" Before Hong-meng's frustration exploded into anger, Lao Tzu quickly added with a smile, "But for you it's a very serious problem, and it doesn't seem to have any solution. Is that correct?" Hong-meng nodded. "Except *that* isn't your problem."

"That isn't my problem?" Hong-meng was shocked at the statement. "What do you mean that isn't my problem? Nobody wants my product. If that isn't my problem, then what *is* my problem?" Hong-meng could no longer hide his anger. The problem was clear. Why was this old man playing games with him?

"Relax!" Lao Tzu instructed, holding up his hand as if to protect himself from Hong-meng's anger. "*He who knows the repose passes little by little from the disturbed to the clear and with movement from the calm to the activity.*" He sat back and lowered his hand as he continued, "Remember what Zhuang Zhu said about listening with your mind and not your ears. You need to think with your mind and not your emotions. Take a deep breath and relax."

Hong-meng inhaled deeply, but he was not relaxed. "How can I relax when you tell me my problem is not my problem?" He folded his arms across his chest. His posture and red face made him look like a small child who had been scolded by his parents. "I'm angry. I think I have a right to be angry. That's normal," he said stubbornly.

"Normal?" Lao Tzu asked in amazement. "First, you have to see that nothing is normal." He waved his hand to show the nothingness that surrounded them. He became more animated as he continued, "Outside the nothingness, the world is never normal. *The world doesn't have norms because the normal can become the abnormal.* The world is never normal; it's always on the edge of abnormal. It's chaotic." Lao Tzu took a deep breath. His eyes lost focus as if he were retreating into himself. After a pause, he continued, "Chaos. That's where it all began. The world began in chaos, and it's always been there. Chaos is the origin."

"What does that have to do with my problem?" Hong-meng asked. He was trying to listen, but he couldn't understand what chaos had to do with his problem—and why normal wasn't normal.

Lao Tzu turned his focus back to the iron tools. "Part of the solution to your problem is in the chaos. Just as part of it is in the nothing."

The shock and confusion on Hong-meng's face made Lao Tzu chuckle. "Chaos and nothing will help me find the solution?" Hong-meng asked, finding it difficult to connect his ears to his mind. His ears heard the words, but they made no sense to his mind.

"Of course," replied Lao Tzu. "First you must understand the problem better. Then you can find the right questions to ask." Before Hong-meng could respond, Lao Tzu asked, "What's your real goal?

"My real goal—" Hong-meng was still confused "—is to find people who want my product, of course," he said, trying to control his anger. He felt as though he'd been repeating the same thing over and over again.

"Hmm," Lao Tzu murmured. "To want—or want to buy?"

"To want to buy, of course."

"To buy? Of course! You didn't say that. To find people who want your product is a different problem from finding people who want to buy your product." Lao Tzu raised his eyebrow in question, as if challenging Hong-meng to disagree.

"Okay. My problem is that I can't find people who want to buy my product," he said. "But I don't see what difference that makes."

"It makes a big difference," stated Lao Tzu. "If we're only interested in them wanting the product, we can just give it to them."

"But I can't do that! I have costs. I have needs. I have a family," Hong-meng replied emphatically. Wasn't it obvious?

"Remember when I told you that *the largest task will be accomplished by small steps?*" Lao Tzu asked. Hong-meng didn't really remember, but he nodded anyway. "If we can define the problem correctly, we can break it down into smaller pieces to solve." Lao Tzu paused to give Hong-meng time to understand. "If we define your problem as 'Nobody wants to buy my product,' then we can break it down into smaller steps and solve each of them."

"Okay, but what do you mean by smaller steps? The problem seems very clear now."

"Yes, I agree. The problem is much clearer now." Lao Tzu raised one finger. "First we know that you have a product with costs. Since you have to support your family, you want to sell it for a profit. You therefore have to define the product and what value it brings. Inside of nothing, there is always something. Hopefully the something has enough value that you can make a profit. Second, once you know what the product is, you need to define who will buy it. Inside of nobody, you need to find the somebody. That only leaves the where and the how."

Hong-meng wondered if it would be rude to get up and go home. He wasn't sure he was going to solve his problem here.

"We already agreed that the world isn't normal," Lao Tzu said. Hong-meng couldn't remember if he'd agreed, but he nodded anyway. "The world is chaotic. The world is made of qi—energy. Qi is constantly regenerating, constantly changing. It's dynamic. You must determine where you can sell your product in a world that isn't static. The people you want to sell to are part of that world. They're constantly changing, irrational, and emotional. They're not static. They're not normal because there is no normal. They are chaos."

Hong-meng nodded helplessly.

Lao Tzu sat quietly and stared off into the nothingness. After a few moments, he said, "I told you that *the voyage of a thousand leagues begins with the first step.*"

"The first step," repeated Hong-meng. He did remember that.

"Yes, the first step. Now we know what the problem is. You want to sell your product for a profit so that you can support your family."

Hong-meng nodded, finally understanding the problem.

"Now we can break the problem into little pieces so it's easier to solve," Lao Tzu continued. "The first step is to find the somewhere hidden in the nowhere. Now we know the first question: where can you sell your product? Where is the market?"

3

THE MARKET

> **It is the form without form.**
> **The image without image.**
> **It is fleeting and elusive.**
>
> —LAO TZU

"According to Tao, in the beginning there was chaos, and from the chaos came order," Lao Tzu stated, waving his hand across the nothingness again. Hong-meng's gaze followed his gesture, trying to see the chaos, but since he didn't know what chaos looked like, he wasn't sure he could see it. Lao Tzu lowered his hand. "The market is also chaos. It has many forms and never seems to have any direction."

"Why?" Hong-meng asked.

"People," Lao Tzu replied seriously.

"People?" Hong-meng asked, surprised. "What do you mean—people?"

"The real market is people," Lao Tzu said simply, as if that were the answer to everything. "It's as simple as that. It's not an abstract entity with convoluted definitions, molded by statistics and demographics. It's simply people. When you understand the motivations of the people, then you will begin to understand your market."

Hong-meng was perplexed. "You said the market is chaos. Now you say the market is people. Do you mean people are chaos?" he asked, trying to connect the two.

Lao Tzu laughed. "Yes, people are chaos. They're irrational, emotional, and always changing their minds. And that's where you need to start when you're looking for your market—in the chaos. Chaos is the beginning, and from chaos comes order."

"That's doesn't make any sense." Hong-meng shook his head. He was beginning to think he'd never find any answers. "Chaos is just chaos. It doesn't have any form. It can't have any order." His voice became louder. "If the market is chaos, then it has no form or order. It's impossible to work with it."

"No, it's not impossible. *The Tao is fleeting and unholdable—it presents an image that is fleeting and unholdable, it is however something.*" Lao Tzu was smiling, as if at a private joke only he knew about. "*It is however something,*" he repeated again. "The real market is like the Tao. You can't really see it or hold it, but it's there. *It is the form without form, the image without image. It is the fleeting and elusive.*"

"If it's without form, and if I can't see it or hold it, how can I find it? And how can I find order in chaos?" Hong-meng was becoming depressed. He was also going crazy. Staring into the nothingness, he saw what appeared to be a man walking toward them.

But he wasn't crazy. Lao Tzu was also watching the man approach. And he wasn't happy. The man was short and stocky, wearing a leather military coat that was broad at the shoulders and padded for protection. As he drew closer, he removed his helmet, revealing a bald scalp. The gray hair at the sides of his head was pulled tightly back and knotted. His beard, which was almost white, hung to the middle of his chest. On his upper lip was a thin, scraggily moustache. He kneeled down so that he completed the triangle between Lao Tzu and Hong-meng. Bowing forward formally, he said in a deep, growly voice, "Greetings, Lao Tzu. It's been a long time."

Lao Tzu glared at the new arrival. He bowed in return and answered, "Hello, Sun Tzu. Time is always too short." His reply was formal but layered in sarcasm.

Sun Tzu laughed, ignoring the sarcasm, and turned to Hong-meng. "Hello, Hong-meng, my name is Sun Tzu," he said in a voice that sounded friendly, but the words were spoken sharply, almost as if he were giving a command instead of a greeting.

"Sun Tzu—the author of the *Bang Fa*—*The Art of War?*" Hong-meng replied, not fully comprehending what was happening. *This had to be a dream,* he thought to himself. This craziness would surely disappear and he would wake up and find his wife snoring quietly next to him and his daughter sitting in the corner of the room, pretending to be quiet but making enough noise to wake up the rest of the house.

"*The Art of War*," grumbled Lao Tzu. He moved back slightly as if to separate himself from the imaginary triangle that held the three of them together.

Sun Tzu chuckled. "That's right. I spent much of my life studying the strategies of some of the most successful generals and brought them all together in one manual—the *Bang Fa*." Turning his gaze to Lao Tzu, he continued, "I overheard your discussions about nothingness, nowhere, nobody, how, and what, and thought Hong-meng could use some practical advice on solving his problem."

"Humph. He's not fighting a war," Lao Tzu retorted, pointing at Hong-meng. "He needs to understand the chaos of his market, the value of his product, and where the real customers are."

"Don't forget about competition, barriers, and gaining a strong position in the market. Marketing is war—you have objectives, territory to capture, and an enemy you need to defeat," replied Sun Tzu, smiling happily at Lao Tzu's discomfort. Hong-meng also felt uncomfortable. Lao Tzu was still pointing toward him and he was beginning to feel that he was the cause of the argument. He also shifted his position in an attempt to move outside the triangle.

Still sulking, Lao Tzu reluctantly lowered his finger and replied sarcastically, "*One observes the world based on their world.*" Sun Tzu remained silent, letting Lao Tzu continue. "The real market doesn't fall into nice little strategies," he said. "It isn't a checklist that can be followed blindly." He stopped suddenly and, after a deep breath, continued in a different tone of voice. His words no longer held their soft persuasion; they became harsher, almost challenging. "It's dynamic and chaotic—it has no beginning and no end. It is so large that you become lost in it. It is so small that you can't see it. It is everywhere and nowhere." He paused again and then added, "*The further one goes the less one knows.*"

"Of course that's true, especially if you don't know where you're going and who the enemy is," Sun Tzu answered sarcastically. "*Thus it is said that one who knows the enemy and knows himself will not be endangered in a hundred engagements.*"

Before Lao Tzu could reply, Hong-meng held up his hand and asked timidly, "And my problem. Have you forgotten about that?" The two older men looked at him in surprise. "Can't we combine your ideas to solve my problem?" he asked with more confidence, glancing from one to the other.

Lao Tzu shrugged and said, "The world began in chaos. Chaos is the origin. Everything starts in chaos. The market is chaos. The beginning is always chaos, with no clear form or direction."

Sun Tzu smiled and, with the confidence of a general, added, "And we need focus, definition, and planning to give chaos form and direction."

Lao Tzu fell silent for a moment and stared down at his hands, which were folded neatly in his lap. Sun Tzu and Hong-meng waited patiently, respecting the silence. Finally Lao Tzu said in a whisper, "Qi." Before Hong-meng could respond, Lao Tzu spoke again in a stronger, more confident voice, "Qi is the energy that drives the market. In the beginning there was chaos, and qi brought form and direction to the world." He paused, almost challenging Sun Tzu to disagree with him, and then went on, "And it's qi that will bring form and direction to the chaos of the market."

Hong-meng wasn't sure he understood what qi had to do with it. "Look into the chaos. Look for the elements that have form. Focus on them." He paused for a moment, thinking about what he'd said. He looked at Lao Tzu. "You said that's the beginning, didn't you? From the chaos comes the beginning. The market is chaos. People are the market, so people are chaos." He wasn't sure he understood what he'd said. He was just repeating what he'd heard. The words didn't really make sense to him. "If I look into the chaos and find the people, aren't *they* what gives the chaos form and direction? What has qi got to do with it?" he asked, looking at the two men for an answer.

Lao Tzu was the first to reply. "Qi is the energy of the market. It is dynamic—constantly changing. If you understand it, you can use it."

Sun Tzu could see the confusion on Hong-meng's face and tried to help. "You're partly right. People are the form. They're your market. It's a very important part, but it's only part of it," he said. "Then *you* have to become part of the market—use it, direct it, control it. That's where the energy of the market becomes important—in the qi of the market, the dynamics of the market."

"If you understand the qi of the market, you can use it to direct and control your particular market," added Lao Tzu, surprised that Sun Tzu agreed with him. "If you don't understand the energy—the dynamics of the market—then you can't control it. Instead, it will control you, and you'll stay lost in the chaos."

"And what do you see in the chaos?" Sun Tzu asked.

"People?" replied Hong-meng, unsure of his answer.

"*Perceive the smallest, that is clairvoyance*," Lao Tzu said.

Hong-meng didn't understand.

"'People' is a big term," explained Sun Tzu. "Which people are you interested in?"

Now Hong-meng understood. "My customers, of course," he said confidently. "The people who will buy my product. The people who will use my product."

Lao Tzu looked pleased. "Excellent. You've identified two layers in the market. Are there any more?"

Hong-meng didn't know he'd identified two layers in the market. He saw the customer as only one layer. Sensing his confusion, Sun Tzu said, "You talked about the person who will buy the product, but you also talked about the person who will use the product. They might be the same person, but not always. Two layers." Hong-meng still looked confused. Sun Tzu continued, "You'll also have another layer—the decision maker. The baron could make the decision on who supplies the tools the peasants will use to farm his land. Someone else might negotiate the price for buying a quantity of your tools. The third layer, the peasant, is the real user. They're all part of your market."

"Exactly," Lao Tzu said, nodding emphatically. "Each layer has different needs and different motivations: the decision maker, the buyer, and the user. They're also driven by different emotions. Each layer is part of your market. You can't ignore any of them. Each has to be convinced to buy your product."

Hong-meng began to grasp the concept. Before, no one wanted to buy his product. Now he was beginning to see the somebody hidden in the nobody.

Lao Tzu cast Hong-meng an approving look. "You're beginning to see something in the chaos."

"But you've only found the form. It still doesn't include order," Sun Tzu added in a serious tone.

Lao Tzu nodded. "Yes, you still need to find the somewhere in the everywhere."

"Somewhere? Everywhere?" Hong-meng was bewildered. "The market is everywhere?"

"Yes, but not your part of the market," Sun Tzu replied, looking over at Lao Tzu for agreement. Seeing a nod from the Taoist sage, he carefully chose his next words. "If you tried to go everywhere, you wouldn't have the time or energy to accomplish anything." After a pause, he added, "*If you expose the army to a prolonged campaign, the state's resources will be inadequate.* You need to know where and who your market is. You must focus."

Picking up the iron plough tip, Lao Tzu asked, "Would you try to sell this to the butcher?" Hong-meng shook his head. "No, of course not. But you'd try to sell the knife to the butcher. And to the farmer." Hong-meng nodded.

Sun Tzu spoke up. "Understanding different market segments means you can focus your resources on those segments where you'll succeed." Seeing Hong-meng's puzzled expression, he tried another tactic to explain what he meant. "*Thus the army values being victorious; it does not value prolonged warfare.* Know where you're going, and you'll be more effective and productive—without wasted time or effort."

Hong-meng thought he understood.

"The market is like a battlefield," Sun Tzu went on. "The great generals always study the battlefield before they commit any troops to battle. Only once they understand the field of battle and have clear objectives will they move. They focus on these objectives. That's their path to victory and success. You must understand your market and what your objectives are, or you'll wander around lost and never succeed."

That's exactly what I've been doing, thought Hong-meng. He was very proud of his small shop. It was always clean and his best tools were displayed outside to attract customers, but he never found any. He would sit outside his shop next to Gai Tie, watching people pass by. He was beginning to understand that these people were not really his customers—they were just people passing by. His customers were people; but not all people were his customers.

"To attack something without form is fruitless," added Lao Tzu reluctantly, uncomfortable with the battlefield analogy. "But to attack everywhere is also fruitless. It's like moving through a dense fog. The direction and objectives quickly get lost."

Hong-meng nodded. "I think I get it. I can see form in the chaos now. I know the customer is a decision maker, a buyer, or maybe a user. Or maybe it's all three, or perhaps something I haven't thought of yet. I also know that only some people will be my customers. I know what my market is now," he said happily, thinking he could go home.

"No, you don't," Lao Tzu disagreed.

"I don't?" Hong-meng asked, confused once again.

"No," Sun Tzu piped in. "You don't know how to position yourself on the battlefield."

Lao Tzu smiled at Sun Tzu's description. "What he means is that you don't know what your position is in the market."

"Yes, I do," replied Hong-meng sadly. "I don't have a position." Depression returned as he reluctantly began to accept the idea that he wasn't going home. He shifted his position on the rocky ground. It seemed this was going to be a long meeting.

"Which means you have to attack to gain a position," Sun Tzu stated, pounding his fist on his knee to emphasize the point. "You have to carve out a position so the enemy has to attack you. You must have a strong position you can easily defend—a home base you can use to expand. *In general, whoever occupies the battleground first and awaits the enemy will be at ease; whoever occupies the battleground afterward and must race to the conflict will be fatigued.*"

Lao Tzu held up his hand before Hong-meng could reply. "That's a very important point," he said, looking down at the iron tools. "Being first in the market can be a significant advantage. The best positions will go to the leader. The follower will always have to take what's left."

"Or he will have to fight the competition to capture the best positions, using energy and resources that could be better used elsewhere," Sun Tzu countered. "Not having to fight is always the best strategy. *Subjugating the enemy's army without fighting is the true pinnacle of excellence.*"

Hong-meng thought about it for a moment. "I can see why being first in the market would be important, and also why having a strong position is important, but what makes a good position and what makes a bad position?"

"I think Sun Tzu already gave two examples of what it takes to have a good position," answered Lao Tzu.

"Exactly. The two most important parts of a good position are that it is easy to defend and you can use it to expand," Sun Tzu replied.

"Having a strong market position, where you are stronger than your competition, means you're not spending all your time defending yourself," Lao Tzu added.

"A good general will always select a position that is easy to defend—the top of a hill, for example, with steep slopes that the enemy must climb to attack," Sun Tzu said. "Your market position—your 'hill'—must create barriers against competition, and at the same time it must give you the ability to attack new markets."

Lao Tzu nodded, showing his agreement with Sun Tzu. "You must have a good, strong defensive position, but that can't be your only goal. If that becomes your sole focus, it becomes like a prison. It keeps the competition out, but it also keeps you locked in. A good market position means you have the time and resources to look at ways to expand." Focusing on Sun Tzu, he continued, "Sun Tzu already said that a good position is one that creates barriers against competition, but if you only focus on your current market position, then you are creating barriers for yourself. You should always be looking for the next step forward. Don't become complacent. Complacency is a dangerous enemy. You should always be looking for ways to improve your position and increase your market."

"Complacency." Hong-meng repeated .

Lao Tzu answered, "Yes. It's too easy to fall into the trap of having a maintenance strategy where you spend all your time defending your past successes. Instead you should always be looking for ways to expand, to incrementally increase your business. You must have a growth strategy."

"That's where you can use qi—the energy of the market—to help drive your growth," added Sun Tzu quietly. "Qi is what drives the market. Every action you take creates this energy, and every action the competition takes also creates this energy. You must manage it to your benefit and, when possible, undermine the qi that helps the competition." Sun Tzu's thoughts drifted back to his old mentor, Wu Tzu-hsu. Wu had always taught that qi was the Tao of a victorious army. Complacency was not part of his vocabulary. He was always driving forward, never satisfied with what he had. Wu knew that a general could be successful only when he understood how to manage and use the qi of his troops. Sun Tzu smiled at the memory. A well-trained army had positive qi. A well-fed army had positive qi. A well-informed army had positive qi. Wu Tzu-hsu understood the value of positive qi, but more importantly, he knew how to create and use it. He also understood that the enemy has its own qi—it has its own energy, its own spirit. Part of Wu's strategy was to turn the enemy's positive qi into negative qi. Attacking the enemy at night with small raiding parties kept them awake and on guard; tired and nervous soldiers have negative qi. Attacking their supply lines instead of the main force meant soldiers were hungry, and hungry soldiers have negative qi. Wu understood that using negative qi could be as effective as an extra thousand soldiers.

Sun Tzu returned his thoughts to the present and said, "If you understand how the market works—if you understand the qi that exists in the market—you can use it to help you succeed and grow."

"If you're complacent—if you're happy with what you have and want nothing more—then the qi can be turned against you and used by your competition," Lao Tzu said in a tone that was almost sad, with a touch of anger mixed in. Lao Tzu knew the dangers of complacency. He'd spent a lifetime traveling through the provinces of Zhou, living among the people and teaching the values of Taoism. He'd become complacent with his own success, and it had blinded him to any belief that might be a threat to his own. It was in the province of Jin on the western borders of the Zhou Empire that he'd first seen Buddhism as a serious threat. His own beliefs had created the energy—the qi—but the Buddhist pilgrims arriving from the west had been able to use that energy against him.

Sun Tzu added, "*Thus one who excels at warfare first establishes himself in a position where he cannot be defeated while not losing any opportunity to defeat the enemy.*"

"How do I get a position that is easy to defend but where I can also expand?" Hong-meng asked.

"To start with, you must find an entry point—a market entry point," Lao Tzu replied.

"And the entry point is where the competition is weak. Is that correct?" he asked.

"Exactly," Sun Tzu said with enthusiasm. "You can use your own strengths to attack their weaknesses. *If we are concentrated into a single force while he is fragmented into ten, then we attack him with ten times the strength.* The enemy isn't going to ignore your threat. You should expect that they'll fight to defend their own positions. You can't assume the competition is going to be complacent. They also want to gain and maintain strong positions in the market."

"Yes," Lao Tzu agreed. "If you can find where your competition is weak, then that is your entry point." He laughed at the thought of the competition lining up in battle formation with swords, spears, and battle chariots, ready to defend their market position. "If you understand your market, you can look for market segments that haven't been fully exploited—new and emerging market segments, for example. You can find the part of the market segment where your competition is weak, perhaps a market segment where your competition has become complacent. You can also look for customers who have become unhappy with the competition. If you can take a competitor's unhappy customer and make him your own happy customer, then that's an easy way to establish a position in the market."

"The market is like a fortified city," Sun Tzu said. "If you're going to attack, you need to know where the weaknesses are in the competition's defences. That's your entry point. You should also identify the best time to attack. When is the window of opportunity? And finally, you need to have a competitive advantage." To emphasize the point, he counted them down using three fingers, "One—the entry point. Two—the window of opportunity. And three—probably the most important for success—your competitive advantage or strength."

"And how do I do that?" Hong-meng asked. Asking questions was easier than giving answers.

Lao Tzu chuckled at Hong-meng's continuing frustration. "Remember I told you that the world wasn't normal—or, at least, what you think is normal can become abnormal?" Hong-meng thought he remembered so he nodded. Lao Tzu continued, "You don't really remember, do you? That's because you didn't believe me. You think your life is normal. It follows the same patterns every day. But hidden in that safe, comfortable, normal life is a desire for change. Normal drives stability. Abnormal creates change."

Sun Tzu spoke up. "The market is the same way—" he glanced at Lao Tzu for confirmation "—it seems to develop patterns that everyone accepts as being normal, just as in your life. But you need change. You need to find the change because that's your entry point into the market. You can wait until something changes and lets you enter the market, or you can be more unorthodox and look for a way to break the normal pattern. *In general, in battle one engages with the orthodox and gains victory through the unorthodox.* To get into the market, normal is your enemy, and change is your friend."

"Think about how we described the market. We said it was chaos," Lao Tzu said before Hong-meng could ask his question.

"But we also said that chaos existed because the market was people," Hong-meng replied.

"Exactly," Sun Tzu said. "People are what create change."

"There are always people who want to break out of the pattern and find something new and better," Lao Tzu added. "*The great path is smooth but the crowd prefers the other trails that cross.* People are chaos. They are emotional and irrational. They want the security of the normal but are always looking for ways to escape into a more exciting life, something different, something better—the abnormal. The chaos of the market can be a barrier, or the abnormal that is always part of chaos can be your path to finding the customer who *prefers the other trails that cross.*"

"Remember, the competition will try to defend the status quo," Sun Tzu continued. "They don't like change. That's their weakness. If you understand your market, you can create the change, and the change will create your entry point. When you understand your strengths and your competitive advantage and can see the weaknesses of the enemy, then change becomes your ally. If the competition has become complacent and is not managing the qi of the market, the market is ready for change. *Do not intercept well-ordered flags; do not attack well-regulated formations. This is the way to control changes.*"

Hong-meng could see how change could become an ally to help him enter the market, but he also understood how strong the defence of the status quo could be. In his home province of Lu, the nobles enjoyed a privileged position and would fight any change that threatened it. But there were also those who welcomed change because they could see it would improve their own position. They were the qi to creating the change. They were the motivation to drive the change. He was sure that the same thing existed in the market. He just had to find it. "And the window of opportunity?" he asked. "How do I know when it's the right time?"

Lao Tzu picked up the iron knife and showed it to Hong-meng. "You already answered that. Your iron tools are your competitive advantage today. When the competition sees that they're better, they'll copy them."

"And then you'll lose your window of opportunity and also your entry point into the market," Sun Tzu said. "You can't wait! *If the enemy opens the door, you must race in!*" He looked over at Lao Tzu before continuing, "You can't wait for the perfect situation. The world is not perfect. You need to make a decision and move quickly or you'll lose the advantage you have and completely miss your window of opportunity. *If someone is victorious in battle and succeeds in attack but does not exploit the achievement, it is disastrous and his fate should be termed 'wasteful and tarrying.'*"

Lao Tzu remained silent. Instead of adding to Sun Tzu's comments, he stared off into the nothingness, lost in his own thoughts. Sun Tzu's enthusiasm slowly eased away and he, too, gazed into the nothingness. Hong-meng watched them both, waiting patiently for them to continue. He thought he understood what they had been telling him, but he still didn't know how that would help him find his customers. Eventually he gave up waiting and asked, "Where's the path through the chaos that will help me find my customer?" He couldn't see anything in the nothingness. Both Lao Tzu and Sun Tzu looked down at the cloth bag next to Hong-meng. "My product *is* the path?" he asked, surprised.

"No," replied Lao Tzu. "Your product will build the path."

"Your product is your competitive advantage," added Sun Tzu. "It is the qi that will help you build the path to find the customers who prefer the other trails. But you need to know how to use it. You must understand the market and know why your product is better—why it can help you find the change you need."

"How can my product build the path?" Hong-meng glanced at his tools.

Lao Tzu laughed and replied, "You don't see the path because you don't know what your product is."

"That's the next question we need to answer—what is your product?" Sun Tzu said.

CHAPTER

4

THE PRODUCT

> **One fashions the clay to make a vase, But it's the emptiness inside that makes it useful.**
>
> —LAO TZU

"We already know what the product is," Hong-meng objected.

"Do we? More importantly, do *you* really know what your product is?" Sun Tzu asked quietly. "*The vanquished army fights first, and then seeks victory*." He emphasized the word *victory*.

"What does that mean?" Hong-meng asked angrily. "Are you trying to tell me that I don't know what my product is?" He glared at Sun Tzu as he reached into his cloth bag and removed the iron tools. He was proud of his work and didn't like being told he didn't have a product.

Lao Tzu raised his hand as if to block the anger, and then said, "I think Sun Tzu is just trying to say that you're selling something before you've really defined what it is. You were looking for answers before you knew what the question was. Now it seems that you're trying to sell something before you really know what it is." He reached over and picked up the knife, turning it slowly in his hand. "You call it a product," he said, looking at it from different angles and testing the sharpness with his finger. "I can see that it's a knife. That's obvious. But what else is it? Is there more?" He stared at the knife as if looking for some hidden secret. Setting it back on the ground, he continued, "Remember, your product is what's going to create the qi in the market to drive change. That's how you're going to get into the market. But it isn't just a product. It has to be more than that." His voice matched the intensity of his look. The knife seemed to glow with a life of its own as he continued, "When you find it, you'll see how it will create your entry point into your market." The glow began to slowly fade away.

Hong-meng examined his products, trying to figure out how they could help create change. They were good. He knew that. He was proud of his work. Every season he watched the farmers bring their broken tools to Meng-ji's workshop for repair. They couldn't afford to buy new tools every year and their bronze tools couldn't survive a season without breaking or losing their sharpness. Because of the poor quality of the existing tools, Meng-ji had a very successful business. Every day he came by Hong-meng's stall to see how many tools he had sold. He knew the iron tools were a threat to his business. The only way he could stay successful was if Hong-meng stayed unsuccessful. But Hong-meng didn't want to stay unsuccessful. He wanted to succeed. How? Even Meng-ji knew his tools could cut and plough better than any bronze tool. He picked up the ax head and looked at it from different angles. Where was the qi that would make the changes he needed to get into the market?

Lao Tzu asked, "What's the value of your product? Where is the real value?" He watched as Hong-meng placed the ax head back on the ground and picked up the plough tip, turning it around and around in his hands, trying to find the real value. Lao Tzu leaned forward and grabbed the knife. He examined it from different angles as if also looking for the real value. Suddenly he held the knife above his head so that the sun reflected off the polished blade. *"One fashions the clay to make a vase, but it's the emptiness inside that makes it useful."* He returned the knife to the ground next to the other tools and, pointing at the plough tip in Hong-meng's hand, stated, "Your plough tip is the vase, but what's the *emptiness*? Where is the real value? What's the real product? What's the value to the customer? Why does he need it? A person may want a vase because it's pretty, but he needs it because of the emptiness. That's where the real value is."

"Why does he need it?" Hong-meng asked himself, looking at the iron plough tip. He stared at it as if the real value would suddenly appear. Finally he gave up. In frustration, he held it out to Lao Tzu as if to prove his point and said, "This is a plough tip. What more do you need to know?"

Lao Tzu took the tool and studied it carefully without any comment.

"Unfortunately, having a good product is not enough," Sun Tzu answered. "Your plough tip is good, but it needs to be better. It has to give the customer some advantage that he can't get from the competition. Remember the barriers." He looked to Lao Tzu as if they were sharing a secret and smiled. "What's the real value of your product?"

"The real value?" Hong-meng again stared at the plough tip, trying to see the *emptiness*. He shook his head and said defensively, "It's made of iron, which means it's harder and stronger than normal bronze tools. It will stay sharper longer and won't break as easily." He sat back and folded his arms across his chest, satisfied with his answer, and waited for Lao Tzu to agree.

Instead Lao Tzu shook his head. "You talk about your product as if it's just a list of features," he said. "And because you think they're good, you automatically think the rest of the world will think the same thing. What is the customer going to see? He's going to see a plough tip, isn't he?" Hong-meng nodded. "Is that all he's going to see? Why should he buy your plough tip instead of using the one he already has?"

Before Hong-meng could answer, Sun Tzu interrupted. "Do you remember when we said that *being unconquerable lies with yourself, being conquerable lies with the enemy?*" He inspected one of the tools more closely. "You're becoming your own enemy. You're creating barriers for yourself."

"What do you mean I'm creating barriers for myself?" Hong-meng was confused. Were they trying to tell him that his products were a barrier?

Lao Tzu answered as if he could hear Hong-meng's thoughts. "No, your products are not the barriers. How you see the products is your barrier."

"Exactly!" Sun Tzu slapped his knee. "Do you remember when Lao Tzu said that *one observes the world based on their world?* That is your barrier. You can only see your product based on your world—or based on comparing it to the competition. You only see the features of your product. Your knife is sharper than the competition's. Your knife is stronger than the competition's. But the real value to the customer is in the product, not just the features. You're so focused on the features that you can't see the value of the whole product. The features are simply a description of the product. They're not a definition of the product. A definition will highlight the values—it will convince the customer that he needs it." He paused for a moment. "A list of features creates want, but a true product definition will show the real value and will create need. Need is better than want! Need is the qi of the market!" He shook his head sadly and added, "You're creating a barrier that blinds you to the real value. You are conquering yourself. You don't need an enemy to do that for you."

Lao Tzu pointed at the iron tool in Sun Tzu's hand. "What is it, really? How would you define it? Why is it good?" He paused, creating a silence that held his small audience in anticipation. "*The goodness is like the water which favorises everyone and is rivalled by nothing*. Where is the goodness of your product? How does it help everyone? Is it so good that it's rivalled by nothing?"

"It's better because it's made of iron," Hong-meng answered defensively but without much confidence.

"Is that all?" asked Lao Tzu. "Is that going to convince your market that they really need your plough tip—just because it's made of iron? Is iron really a competitive advantage? Or is it just different? Different isn't always an advantage. Being different can scare off your customers."

Sun Tzu stepped in. "Remember that we want change—not difference. People don't like being different. Different is dangerous—it isolates people from the rest of society. When you hear someone say they're different, it's usually not said as a compliment. Change is your ally. People like change if it improves their lives and improves their standing among their neighbors. Difference is the enemy. Differences will be used by the competition to help defend the status quo. Being different becomes another barrier to entering the market."

"To get into the market, you have to convince the customers that they need *your* plough tip and not the competition's," Lao Tzu added. "People don't need something different. They need something that gives them an advantage over what they have now." He paused, watching Hong-meng nod. "Need and competitive advantage! Those are the tools you need to break down the barriers," he said slowly, trying to emphasize the point. "Do you remember how we described your market and how we can find those who need a plough tip? The something in the nothing, the somewhere in the nowhere, and the somebody in the nobody. Now you have to convince them that they *need* your iron plough tip."

"Look at your ax head," Sun Tzu said, pointing at the tool next to Hong-meng. "Tell me about it."

Hong-meng picked up the ax head and turned it in his hand, trying to see what made it special. "It's sharp and it won't break easily. Bronze tools lose their edge quickly and break easily." He knew it wasn't the correct answer, but he didn't know what else to say.

Lao Tzu shook his head. "You're still just listing the features. You're describing the vase, but you still don't see the real value—the *emptiness*." He pointed at the tool. "Need, competitive advantage, and value to the customer. Where are they? You must look at your product as if you are the customer. What does the customer see? The customer should see need; he should see a unique value for himself and should have the perception that it is better than any other tool he could get." Trying to prompt Hong-meng, Lao Tzu added, *"Only those for whom life isn't too hard can appreciate life."* He could tell Hong-meng didn't understand. "Does it make your customer's life easier? Or is there no advantage in changing? Remember, you must overcome the obstacles. Why should they change? Is the bronze ax that they're using today making their life harder? Why should he throw away the bronze ax and buy yours?" Lao Tzu took a deep breath. "Imagine a customer who has three ax heads in front of him. One is yours and the other two are from your competition. Why should he choose yours?"

Hong-meng looked back and forth from Lao Tzu to Sun Tzu, trying to think of something to say. Unfortunately, his mind was confused and filled with empty thoughts.

"Remember the vase," Sun Tzu said, trying to help. *"It's the emptiness inside that makes it useful.* The real value of the vase is its emptiness."

Lao Tzu waved his hand across the ground, and two ax heads appeared next to the iron tool. The new ones were both made of bronze. One was large with a very thick blade, obviously made for heavy work. The second was smaller with a narrow, thick blade and intricately cut designs along the base where the wooden handle fit. "They're all ax heads. Now imagine that you're a customer and you already have this one." He pointed at the large bronze ax head. "Why would you change?"

Hong-meng reached over and picked up the large bronze ax head. Examining it closely, he could see that it had already seen a lot of use. It needed sharpening and the chips in the blade needed to be ground away or they would become deeper. He'd seen this type of situation many times before. He'd watched farmers going to Meng-ji's shop to get their tools repaired. He'd see the damage on the bronze tool and explain to the owner that it wouldn't happen with his iron tools, but it didn't seem to make any difference. He couldn't convince them to buy a new tool; it was easier and less expensive just to repair the old ones. Hong-meng didn't know what to say.

"You're the customer," Lao Tzu reminded him. "Why would you change?"

"If I were the customer," Hong-meng said, talking more to himself than to the others, "I would be unhappy that I have to have the ax head repaired and sharpened."

"Why?" asked Sun Tzu.

"Because I have to stop work to take it to Meng-ji and then wait while he repairs all the chips in the blade and sharpens it." Hong-meng held out the large bronze ax head to Sun Tzu. "Since it's easily damaged, I also lose valuable working time. And since it doesn't stay sharp, I have to work harder to accomplish the same amount of work."

"Does that mean you would consider changing to another product?" Lao Tzu asked.

"Of course," Hong-meng replied. "If I could become more productive and not lose working days, I would consider changing."

"And with a tool that would stay sharp, you wouldn't have to work so hard to finish the job, would you?" Sun Tzu stated. Hong-meng smiled.

"I think you understand now," Lao Tzu said. "Do you see the difference between the features of your product and the definition of your product—a definition that creates need?"

"Yes, I think I do," Hong-meng replied. "My product increases productivity, and that means my customers don't have to work as hard to accomplish the same amount of work."

"I think you understand," Sun Tzu said. "The fact that your iron ax head stays sharp longer and doesn't break as easily as the bronze tools are nice features, but if the customer doesn't need them, they don't have any real value. By defining the product correctly, you can show how the features create real value for your product and convince the customer that they need it. If the iron tools stay sharp and don't break, it means higher productivity and more efficiency. The features have now become a product definition that has real value to the customer." He paused to make sure he had Hong-meng's attention. "You've found the value and created need."

"What about this ax head?" Sun Tzu asked as he picked up the bronze tool with the engraving on the side.

"That's easy," replied Hong-meng, feeling more confident. "The engraving doesn't add value to the product. It creates want but not need."

"Are you sure?" Sun Tzu asked. Even Lao Tzu looked surprised at the question.

"It's a bronze ax head, just like the other one," Hong-meng answered defensively. "Why should it be any different just because it has engraving?"

"With your current product definition, you're right," Sun Tzu said, looking at Lao Tzu for support. The surprise on Lao Tzu's face was slowly replaced with a nod of support as he began to understand what Sun Tzu was trying to say.

"You said that the engraving didn't add any value to the product," Lao Tzu said. "Is that really true? You created a definition of your product from its features, which showed why the customer would need it. Isn't that correct?" he asked. Hong-meng nodded but remained silent, not sure what direction the conversation was headed in. "There's another feature of your product that you've forgotten about—one you could use in your product definition to add value and create additional need."

Hong-meng looked at his tools, trying to see what other feature was. "What feature?"

"You," replied Sun Tzu. "You are the feature."

"Yes, you." Lao Tzu smiled at Hong-meng's disbelief. "It's simple, Hong-meng. You are a master craftsman. Your skill adds value to the product. You need to add that value into your product definition."

Hong-meng thought about the idea. "But the quality is already built in. How do I use it to add value?"

Sun Tzu smiled and pointed at the ax head with the engraving.

"Engraving?" Hong-meng asked, even more confused. "How will that help add value? It will only make the product look prettier. It doesn't make it function any better."

"Wrong," Sun Tzu barked, becoming impatient with Hong-meng. "It creates an image. Tools that are marked with the Hong-meng brand will be immediately recognized as quality tools. It creates additional value."

"Don't underestimate the value of branding," Lao Tzu said. "It's another way for you to establish a stronger position in the market." Sun Tzu nodded. "If branding is part of the product definition, if it adds to the customer's value of the product and isn't just decoration, then it'll help create the qi in the market so that you can expand."

"Not only will it add to the value of your product, but it'll create barriers for the enemy," Sun Tzu said. "If you can define your products so that they have a strong image in the market, it will be more difficult for the competition to attack your position. If you've already created the need for your products, then branding can add another layer of value. However, it won't work if you try to use branding before you've created the need. Branding without need is just a pretty product." He gestured to the engraved ax head. He could see that Hong-meng was thinking about what he'd said, but he repeated it just to make sure the message was clear. "Create extra value for your customers and, at the same time, establish a stronger market position. It's definitely an important part of your product definition." He emphasized the words *product definition*.

Hong-meng got the message, but before he could say anything, Sun Tzu raised the ax head. "That's what you need to do with your other tools." He indicated the tools on the ground. "Identify the real value and use it to define your products so that they'll meet the needs of the customer. Compared to the competition, each tool will meet some minimum definition—a knife is a knife—but it's the *emptiness* that's really important. Find the *emptiness*. That's the real value. What you've done with your product to enhance the features and make it better than the competition is important, but these enhanced features need to become part of the product definition. When you can define the real value of your product to the customer, that's where you'll find your competitive advantage."

Hong-meng took the ax head from Sun Tzu. For the first time, he began to see his product differently. Instead of seeing all the features that he had produced, he began to see its value from a customer's point of view. Maybe he was finally beginning to understand. Before, he'd always defined his product from his own perspective, one that could only see the features. He'd never really thought about the customer. The technical features were still important and he was proud of what he'd accomplished, but now he knew how to use them to create value. They were like pieces in a puzzle. He could put them together to build a picture in which the customer could see the value. They weren't interested in the technical features; all they wanted to know was how the product would help them. They wanted to know why they *needed* it. It was beginning to make sense why he hadn't been able to convince customers to buy his products. He'd focused only on why his products were better and not on the value they would give his customers. He hid the real value behind technical details; he had focused only on the want and never on the need.

Sun Tzu picked up the knife and inspected it as if he, too, were looking for the value hidden behind the features. To show that he had learned the lesson, Hong-meng began to define the knife, but Sun Tzu held up his hand and asked, "Can I see the other types of knives you have?"

"That's the only one. Why?" Hong-meng asked suspiciously. "What's wrong with it?"

"The sword that is sharpened unendingly, cannot conserve its edge for a long time," replied Lao Tzu.

"My knife will hold an edge for a long time," Hong-meng said defensively.

"I'm sure it will," he answered. "Listen with your mind, Hong-meng. What is the message behind the words?" He could see that Hong-meng had only heard the words, not the meaning. "How many customers can you find with this knife? Do you remember when we talked about knowledge?" Hong-meng nodded, but he wasn't really listening. He was still staring at his knife to see why it *cannot conserve its edge for a long time*. "We said that existing knowledge was the biggest obstacle to finding new knowledge. Isn't that right?"

"Yes, I remember," Hong-meng replied. "What does that have to do with my knife?"

"It has two things to do with all your tools, not just the knife," Lao Tzu said. "First, you now know the importance of defining your products so that you focus on the value and the customer's need. That knowledge is now blocking you from seeing how you can expand the value even further. You think you have enough knowledge and you're ready to go home. Is that right?"

Hong-meng was embarrassed. That was exactly what he was thinking.

Lao Tzu continued, "This knowledge should only be the first step to more knowledge. Knowledge should have no beginning and no end. *The end and the beginning are things that begin without end. The beginning of one is the end of the other, the end of one is the beginning of the other.*" He paused, enjoying Hong-meng's obvious frustration and embarrassment.

Before he could continue, Sun Tzu interrupted. "We already talked about the market—how it's dynamic, always changing. Your products need to be the same. Static products die quickly in a dynamic market. *One who cannot be victorious assumes a defensive position; one who can be victorious attacks.* You need to look at how your products can evolve to survive and how you can continue to add even more value so that your market position becomes even stronger and you can expand even further."

"My products need to evolve?" Hong-meng asked.

"Exactly! That leads us to the second point I talked about," Lao Tzu answered. "This new knowledge you've gained is blocking you from seeing how your products can evolve. It's blocking innovation."

"What do you mean?" Hong-meng replied defensively.

Sun Tzu picked up the discussion. "Innovation can create the qi to help you expand in the market." Hong-meng started to ask a question, but was interrupted by Sun Tzu. "Creativity is the ability to find new ideas. It's part of the qi that will help you get into and establish yourself in the market. But we also said that one of the dangers of having a strong position is complacency. You must look at ways to expand. Innovation is the ability to move existing ideas into the future, making them better. It is a continuous regeneration. The regeneration will only happen if you can look beyond today and not get trapped in the past." He knew what was on Hong-meng's mind. "Many people are so focused on the past that they can't see past today," he added. "They see what the competition has already done and try to improve it. That's not real innovation. Innovation should be part of the future and not part of the past. If you can use innovation to move you past today, it will become the qi to help you expand in the future. It's the next step in the definition of your product."

Lao Tzu smiled at Hong-meng. "Creativity has a certain amount of risk, since it means exploring new territory," he said. "Most people are scared of creativity because they are scared of the unknown. That's why many craftsmen and shop owners don't want to be first in the market. They prefer to be followers and let someone else take the risks. Even though the obstacles to entry might be lower, the risks are going to be very much higher—and they don't like risk. Innovation is different. It has less risk, since it's starting from a known position, but it can be just as important."

"And what does this have to do with knowledge?" Hong-meng asked. The conversation seemed to be going around in circles.

Lao Tzu held up the knife to emphasize his point. "You understand now how to define the value of this knife, but that knowledge is blocking you from expanding the definition to include more. You're satisfied with your definition and you're not looking for more. You're not looking beyond your current knowledge. You've become complacent."

"There is a master in Qufu, Kong Fu Tzu, who teaches that *he who learns but does not think, is lost,*" Sun Tzu said. "You've shown that you are able to learn, but you also need to think. Step back and try to become the customer again. What does the customer use the knife for?"

"There are lots of uses for a knife," Hong-meng said angrily.

"But you have only one type of knife," Lao Tzu replied, ignoring the anger in Hong-meng's voice.

"You need to have a family of knives," Sun Tzu quickly clarified, trying to get Hong-meng to concentrate on the conversation and not on his anger and frustration. "You must create a family of knives so that you can expand your market presence—so that you'll meet more than one need of your customer. That's where you can use innovation to help create additional product value—and additional sales."

"Then your customer will buy several knives from you, each one for a different need," Lao Tzu said. "Also, each time you deliver a new kind of knife, you create a new barrier for the competition. They won't know where you're going to attack next." He glanced at Sun Tzu for support.

"The location where we will engage the enemy must not become known to them," Sun Tzu said. "The definition of the product is your weapon to attack the market and establish a position. And that's only the beginning. You must always look for the next step. By adding to your family of products, you create barriers for the competition. They don't know what you're going to do next."

Hong-meng could see the advantage of having several types of knives, or plough tips, or any other tool, but how would he know which ones were important? Having a shop full of different knives that the market didn't want didn't seem like a good idea. "How do I know what these other tools are?"

"Use the qi of the market," Lao Tzu replied. "It will tell you what innovation you need to build your family of products."

Hong-meng thought for a minute. "But you said the market was people."

"Exactly! It's that simple—ask your customers what they need," Lao Tzu answered, laughing. "Don't you remember that I told you that the answer was easy to find if you ask the right question?" Hong-meng nodded, but he wasn't sure if he'd asked the right question. Lao Tzu continued, "You asked 'How do I know what these tools are?' That was the wrong question, wasn't it?"

Hong-meng understood. "I should've asked *who* can tell me what tools I need. Then the answer is obvious—my customers." Hong-meng was silent for a moment. "How do I find the customers to ask what they need?"

Lao Tzu held up the knife. "This is the key that will open the door to the market—your lead product. If you've defined it correctly, then you'll find your customers. You'll also find that customers are very strange. They're chaotic, always changing their minds. They always say, 'I like it, but…' That's when they'll tell you what other products they need."

"When you listen to the market and know how to use innovation to meet the needs of your customers, you're beginning to understand how to use the qi of the market," Sun Tzu said seriously.

Hong-meng felt he was finally beginning to understand the qi of the market. "You said the customer is strange. What do you mean?"

"That's the next small step in solving your problem," Sun Tzu replied. "The next question is: what is the customer?"

CHAPTER

5

THE CUSTOMER

> The more one speaks of it
> The less one can hold it.
>
> —LAO TZU

"What is the customer?" Hong-meng was surprised by the question. "I thought the customer was a user, a buyer, or a decision maker. Is that wrong?"

"No, that's not wrong, but that's only part of it," Sun Tzu answered. He was staring at the tools, but not really seeing them. "What is the customer? A buyer, a user, a decision maker? Yes, that's probably a good definition, but that's only part of the question. The question is bigger than that."

"Sun Tzu is absolutely right," Lao Tzu said. "The customer is more than just somebody who buys your product. A customer can help you protect your market by creating barriers to the competition. A customer can open new markets so that you can expand your business. A customer can also be a source of innovation for new products." Lao Tzu raised his hand so that Hong-meng could see the small rock he was holding. "Imagine this rock is your customer. To see it properly, you must look with both eyes. If you look with only one eye, you begin to lose a lot of the detail and many of the key features disappear. They aren't as clear as they were and the contours aren't as strong. It's almost as if it becomes two-dimensional."

Hong-meng closed one of his eyes. Lao Tzu was right. He could still tell that it was a rock, but a lot of the surface details had disappeared and the shape and contours weren't as clear.

"If you look at the rock with both eyes, all the surface details and the contours come back," Lao Tzu continued. Hong-meng opened both eyes and the contours of the rock appeared again. "Even more important, if you turn the rock around, you can see new sides of it." Lao Tzu held up the rock in front of his face and closed one eye. "You must understand how to look at the rock so that you can see all the features and know what it really is." The rock disappeared from his hand.

"How you see your customer is very similar to how you see the rock," Sun Tzu interrupted. "If you only use one eye, then the customer seems simple—someone who only buys your product. But if you use both eyes and look at him from different angles, you will see that the real customer is very complex and multidimensional. That's when we see that 'What is the customer?' is only part of the question. To see and understand the real customer, we must look beyond the simple 'what.' The question must also be 'Who is the customer?' and 'How do you find your customer?'" He looked at Lao Tzu. "What? Who? How? We have three questions to answer, not just one."

"If the customer is a user, buyer, or decision maker, and we can find him hidden in the chaos of the market," Hong-meng said hesitantly, "then doesn't that answer the questions?" He hoped he was right. He wanted to go home and the last thing he needed was another voyage into the confusing world of nothing, nowhere, and nobody.

"Hmm. In the chaos of the market," Lao Tzu repeated, nodding. "The chaos is like a thick fog, distorting and hiding the customer. Who is the customer? The customer becomes hidden in this fog of chaos." He gestured to the nothingness that surrounded them. "You can only see vague shapes and shadows. It's like looking for the something in the nothingness. You're looking for something where there seems to be only a world of changing shadows."

Hong-meng hung his head in disappointment. He knew he wasn't going home yet.

"That's why you need to clear away the fog. You'll end up chasing every shadow, hoping that it's a real customer." Sun Tzu noticed the disappointment on Hong-meng's face but didn't understand it.

"How can I find my customer if I can only see shadows?" Hong-meng asked without much confidence, looking at Lao Tzu for help.

Instead of replying, Lao Tzu smiled as if he were waiting for Hong-meng to find his own answer. Hong-meng understood Lao Tzu's silence and forced himself to concentrate on trying to find the answer. He knew it was buried there somewhere but he couldn't see it, and the more he tried, the more nervous he became.

Sun Tzu watched Hong-meng struggle, but since patience wasn't one of his strong points, he interrupted the silence. "That might be easier than you think." He ignored Lao Tzu's frown. "It's useless to chase every shadow. What you need to do is convince the customer to come to you. Instead of pushing your way into the fog, pull the customer out. Get the customer to come to you. *In order to cause the enemy to come of their own volition extend some apparent profit.*"

"You said the enemy. Does that mean the customer is the enemy? Is that really true?" Hong-meng had never thought of his customers as being his enemy.

"Sometimes you'll think so," Sun Tzu answered, laughing at Hong-meng's expression. "Maybe 'a reluctant ally' would be another way of describing them. At least that's what you want. At first, they'll always seem like the enemy. You need to find and convince these potential enemies to become your allies."

Lao Tzu was frowning. It was obvious from his expression that he didn't like describing the customer as an enemy. "A customer is like the market—dynamic and constantly changing. Customers are people, and because they're people, they're irrational, emotional, and stubborn." Lao Tzu wasn't sure Hong-meng followed his thought, but he continued anyway. "We already talked about how qi can help you manage your market. You also have to be able manage your customers. Customers go through various stages, and you have to manage them so that you end up having a good customer."

"Is that how I change the customer from an enemy to an ally?" Hong-meng asked.

"Yes," Lao Tzu replied reluctantly, still not liking the term *enemy*. "Except that a customer has more than two stages. In the first stage they are not really an enemy. 'Suspicious' would probably be a better description. They are suspicious because they don't see any value to your product and they don't trust your motivations for trying to sell it to them. Why should they change from what they already have? This is why your product definition is so important—the *apparent profit*. If you've defined your product correctly, they'll be able to see the benefit and will come out of the fog. Then they move to the next stage—the interested stage."

"As soon as your customers reach the interested stage, they are no longer vague shadows. They become real." Sun Tzu paused. "No, that's not true," he said, correcting himself. "They're still only potential customers, but at least they're no longer shadows. You know who they are and you can identify them as a real opportunity. The real customer comes in the next stage."

"So now I've found a potential customer. He's no longer hidden in the fog of chaos," Hong-meng said hesitantly. "What do I do next? What are the next stages? How do I find my real customer?"

Lao Tzu sensed Hong-meng's frustration. "*The more one speaks of it the less one can hold it.* We warned you that the customer is complex. It's not always easy to find the real customer."

"What's a real customer?" Hong-meng asked. He agreed with the idea that *the more one speaks of it the less one can hold it*. It seemed that the more they talked about the customer, the more complex it became.

"A real customer is someone who buys your product," Sun Tzu replied. "But they're also the people who help strengthen your market position and help you grow." Hong-meng looked confused again. He thought a real customer was simply one who needed his product and was willing to pay for it. As if he could hear Hong-meng's thoughts, Sun Tzu said, "You're right. A customer is someone who needs your product and is willing to pay for it. But we already said that a customer is more than just that. A real customer is someone who has confidence in you. He understands the real value of your product. He feels that he is getting value for his money. That's why you have to win his confidence by showing some real value. Then you'll attract the real customers. Customers are always going to be suspicious. You need to reassure them. Showing them how they can *profit* from your product is the best way to do so."

"What kind of profit?"

"Meeting their needs is a key part of the profit that will attract them," Sun Tzu replied. "If you can find and meet that need, the suspicious customer will see the real value of your product and the benefits that it gives him. Need, value, and benefit are the elements of profit that will pull him out of the fog and move him into the next stage—the interested customer. That's why your product definition is so important. It's the qi—the force that will pull the suspicious customer out of the fog of chaos and create interest. A list of product features will not do that. The customer needs to see a benefit that is strong enough to make him want to change."

Lao Tzu chimed in. "Do you remember Zhang Zhou? He was the wind that explained that you needed to listen with your mind and not your ears." Hong-meng nodded. "He has another saying: *one forgets his feet when one has comfortable shoes.* Your potential customers hidden in the fog of chaos are the ones who think they have comfortable shoes. They think they're happy with what they have. Your product definition needs to convince the suspicious customer that his 'feet' are not really comfortable with his current ax head or plough tip. Your product needs to drive the qi of the market to create the change." Lao Tzu was silent for a moment. "We need a customer who is more than just interested. We need a customer who will buy your product. We need a satisfied customer."

"The satisfied customer is the next stage?" Hong-meng guessed.

"Yes," Lao Tzu replied. "The satisfied customer is the third stage. He will buy your product because it satisfies his needs."

"The satisfied customer will be your real customer," Sun Tzu said. "Remember when we talked about what the customer is? We talked about the different layers in the market. Or we talked about the user, the buyer, and the decision maker. Each layer is a potential customer—an interested customer. But each has a different need. You not only have to find the need for each layer, but you also have to determine whether the decision maker is a separate layer, as we said before, or whether he is part of the other layers. Where is the real decision being made? The interested customer will not become a satisfied customer if he's not the decision maker. The decision maker may not be a separate layer at all. He may be part of the other layers. You have to convince all the layers, but without convincing the decision maker, you will never have a real customer."

Hong-meng was becoming increasingly depressed. It was all very confusing. He thought a customer should be someone who needed and bought his product. Instead of being simple, it was becoming very complicated. A customer could be a potential customer, a real opportunity, a real customer, a suspicious customer, an interested customer, or a satisfied customer—and, to make it even worse, there were different layers of customers, each with his own needs. Hidden somewhere in there was someone called a decision maker. To shake off his confusion, he began thinking out loud. "My customers are hidden in the chaos of the market. They're like shadows drifting through a thick fog. To pull these customers out of the fog of chaos, I need to have a strong product definition where the real value of my products will overcome their suspicions of what my intentions are and make them interested. But these two stages are just potential customers. If my product definition is good enough, the interested customer will see that he needs my product and he will buy it. Then he becomes a real customer—a satisfied customer." He paused, thinking about what he'd said. "Is that right? Have I listened with my mind and not just my ears?" He couldn't help smiling.

"A satisfied customer is a critical stage in the management of your customers," Lao Tzu answered. "If you are successful in that stage, you will increase your sales and expand your market. Then you can transform a satisfied customer into a loyal customer—the next stage. From there, it's a small step to create a repeat customer." He knew Hong-meng wanted to ask the obvious question. "Why should we bother having a stage for the loyal customer? Is that what you were going to ask? A repeat customer will bring more sales. That should be our focus." Hong-meng started to say something, but Lao Tzu interrupted. "Don't underestimate the value of having a loyal customer. We already said that a customer is more than just someone who buys your product. A loyal customer will help build barriers to stop your competition. They're also the customers who will tell you what innovation you need for new products so that you can expand your market. It's an important stage for strengthening your market position and growing. If you ignore that stage, a loyal customer can quickly become unsatisfied and disappear. Then he becomes a weakness the competition can use."

"Your loyal customers are important to build a strong market position," Sun Tzu repeated, emphasizing the point. "They are your defence against attack by the competition. They also give you the opportunity to expand your market. If you put effort into taking care of your loyal customers, they can easily be moved to the next stage—the repeat customer."

"Then I can increase my sales," Hong-meng said.

Lao Tzu laughed. "Yes, but you still have one important stage. When you have a satisfied customer who is loyal and comes back when he needs to buy other tools, you can move the customer to the last stage—the promoter."

"What's that?" Hong-meng asked.

"A promoter is a satisfied, loyal, repeat customer who is very happy with your products. They meet his needs and he can clearly see their real value. He is so impressed with your products that he recommends and promotes them to others. He helps you sell your tools. Don't underestimate the value of having someone else who will sell your products for you. Having a larger army than the enemy is always a strategic advantage."

"How do I find a customer who will help me sell my tools?" Hong-meng asked with genuine interest. He liked the idea that others would help him sell his products.

"You need to understand your customers," Lao Tzu answered simply. "We've now answered the question, 'What is the customer?' He's the user, the buyer, and the decision maker. We've also answered, 'Who is the customer?' He's the different stages: suspicious, interested, satisfied, loyal, repeat, and promoter. Now we need to answer the last question: how do you find your customers?"

Hong-meng thought the answer was that the customer is in the chaos of the market, but he knew that was too simple.

"Think about what it was like trying to sell your tools," Sun Tzu said. "Did you find interested or satisfied customers? Or did you only find suspicious ones?"

Hong-meng looked embarrassed. "You're right. I was desperate," he said, bitterness apparent in his voice. "I'd try to sell them to anyone who would listen."

"You never qualified your customers," Lao Tzu replied. "You thought of your customer as a simple, single stage, and you never tried to separate the curious from the real customer."

Hong-meng wasn't happy with the truth, but he had to agree. He thought back to the times he'd tried to sell his iron tools to every person who visited his shop. A lot of them were just curious and weren't interested in buying tools of any kind, but he still wasted his time trying to sell to them. And the others? What about the ones who could've been real customers? They always stayed at the suspicious stage because he only used the features of the product to convince them. He never showed them the real value of his products. They didn't need his products because they never saw the benefits. He said to Lao Tzu, "And the customers—the potential customers—they already seemed to be happy with the tools they had. I wasn't able to convince them they needed my tools."

Lao Tzu nodded. *"He who is content with himself will always have enough.* They were only potential customers because you never really understood what their needs were. *Because he is disinterested, his own interests are preserved.* You couldn't break through their disinterest. They thought they were happy with what they had. You never made them your customers because you never convinced them they'd be happier with your tools. They stayed hidden in the fog because you never really understood them—or their real needs."

Hong-meng looking from Lao Tzu to Sun Tzu and back again. "How do I understand them? They're strangers."

"One observes others based on oneself," replied Lao Tzu, laughing.

Hong-meng was trying to listen with his mind, but it wasn't working. Sun Tzu could see the frustration on Hong-meng's face and held up a polished metal disk—a mirror. "What do you see, Hong-meng?" he asked seriously.

"I see me," Hong-meng answered, seeing his face reflected in the polished disk. He knew immediately that it was the wrong answer, but it was too late to change it.

"No," stated Lao Tzu. "You see only a reflection of you. You don't see the real you. It's the same when you look at your customers. You only see a reflection of the customer—a reflection that comes from your own motivations and ego. You're not seeing the real customer. You're already convinced that your tools are better, and when you look at the customer, you assume they can also see the value. The reflection is getting in the way of reality." He tossed the metal disk out into the nothingness. "You need to get rid of the mirror. You need to see what is real and not just reflection. Then you can see the real need, the real motivation, the *profit* that will attract the real customers."

Hong-meng was struggling with the idea. Sun Tzu tried to help by adding, "Maybe the first step in trying to understand your customers is to understand yourself. It's clear you're very proud of your work," He pointed at the row of tools on the ground. "But your own ego and pride is always going to get in the way of trying to understand your customers."

"He who knows others is intelligent. He who knows himself is enlightened," Lao Tzu said.

"I need to be enlightened?" Hong-meng was beginning to feel that making the tools was easy compared to trying to sell them. When he made them, he was working with facts he could see and understand—how much heat to form the metal, how much carbon to add at the correct time. It was a process with clearly defined steps. Selling the tools was a completely different world. He didn't have any real facts to work with. Instead he was working with abstract concepts like chaos, emotion, need, satisfaction, and value. Now he had to add enlightenment to the list. There didn't seem to be any beginning or any end to it. *"It is the form without form. The image without image. It is fleeting and elusive."*

"If you understand your own bias and preconceptions, you can filter them out and not be confused by the reflections," Lao Tzu explained.

Hong-meng was feeling more confident. "If I can filter out my own motivations, my preconceptions, my pride and ego, then I can see the real customer.

I can see beyond the reflection and I know where my customer is. Is that what you're saying?"

"Yes, but that's not all," replied Sun Tzu. Hong-meng shook his head. Would he ever really understand? Sun Tzu continued, "The problem is that even if you can get past the reflection, you still have to be careful that you're seeing what's really there." Sun Tzu pointed at the sky. "Do you see the sun?"

"Of course," he answered impatiently.

"No, you don't," Lao Tzu countered. "You only see the light of the sun. The sun creates light, but it's not made of light."

Hong-meng looked up at the sun. His mind was beginning to connect the ideas together. "I see it, but I don't see what it really is."

"Just like the customer. The real customer is not that easy to find," Lao Tzu admitted, watching Hong-meng struggling with the idea. "*The more one speaks of it the less one can hold it.* We've already seen how your pride and ego can hide customers behind a reflection of what you think they are. You need to get rid of the reflection. But you also have opinions, don't you?" he asked. "Your opinions are the light of the sun. They blind you from seeing what is really there. Your own opinions about your product are going to be a major obstacle to understanding your customer. How many times have you lost your temper because the 'stupid' customer didn't buy your product? Your product was better than all the others. That was obvious—at least to you. Not to the customer! You couldn't get past your own opinions. Your opinion of your own product blinded you to the *disinterest* of the customer."

Hong-meng thought back to what Lao Tzu had said earlier: *one observes others based on oneself.* "So if I can understand who I really am, my own motivations and my own needs, and not be deceived by the reflection in the mirror and also not be blinded by the 'light' of my opinions, then I can use that same ability to see who my customers really are? Determine their likes and dislikes, their motivations, and their real needs? Is that what you're trying to say?"

"Exactly! We said you had to meet the needs of the customer, but you have to be able to see those needs first." Sun Tzu slapped his hand on his knee. "If you don't understand your own motivations, likes, and dislikes, they'll end up getting in the way and biasing your understanding of your customers. It was the same when you tried to define your product. All you could see were the features. They were getting in the way of finding the real value." His tone of voice became authoritative. "Focus on the customer, find his need, and use the need to attract him. Then change his disinterest to interest."

Before anyone could say anything more, the wind picked up. Hong-meng again heard the voice, this time saying, *"Life is like a galloping horse, each of its movements is a change in form and a change in place."*

Sun Tzu looked confused. Lao Tzu laughed. "That was Zhuang Zhou. He is—or at least he will be in another hundred seasons—a prolific but very cynical Taoist monk."

"What was he saying?" Sun Tzu was still confused by the interruption.

Lao Tzu started to reply, but Hong-meng raised his hand as if he were a student in class requesting to speak. "He was reminding me that to really understand the customer, I must understand that he is part of a market that is always changing—like a galloping horse." He looked at Lao Tzu and added, "The market is dynamic. It's made up of people. People are the real customers, and they're always changing."

"Yes, they're always changing," Lao Tzu repeated. "Change is good. Change is the qi to help you enter the market." He paused, using the silence to add a layer of importance to his next statement. "If you understand your customer, you will be able to see the power of change and be able to use it. But you should never underestimate the power of change. As soon as you think you understand your customer, everything will change again—just like the galloping horse." He smiled even though his tone was serious. *"If the people are difficult to govern, it is because of an excess of intelligence.* Never underestimate the capabilities of your customer."

He reached down and picked up the iron knife. Looking at Hong-meng, he asked, "Where is your customer? You know your customers are going to be hidden in the fog of chaos that makes up the market. To find your real customers and not waste time chasing every shadow, you need to understand their needs and use that to attract them. A reflection of the customer is not the real customer. You must look beyond the light to see what is really there. Each type of customer—the user, buyer, and decision maker—has different needs. When you find those needs, a suspicious customer can be converted through the stages to become a happy promoter customer. That becomes your strength." He paused, watching Hong-meng's reaction. "When *the people no longer fear your power…it is because a greater power approaches."*

"A greater power?" asked Hong-meng.

"The competition is the greater power," Sun Tzu clarified. "That's the next question. Who is the competition? How do you handle it?"

CHAPTER

6

THE COMPETITION

> **There is no worse danger than to underestimate your enemy.**
>
> —Lao Tzu

Hong-meng was depressed again. "I have lots of competition," he said as he thought of the small, winding alley near the main market where his shop was. Like many cities in the Zhou Empire, the market was located outside the protection of the inner city walls, where the duke and the rich merchants lived in luxurious isolation. As business in the city increased, the marketplace grew in size and importance, with skilled artisans and craftsmen separating themselves from the turmoil and chaos of the open market by setting up shop in the winding side streets. The various artisans that provided the city with its goods began to congregate in the same streets, so that you had streets dedicated to pottery, woodworking, and tools. Which meant that Hong-meng's neighbors were also his competitors—and he had a lot of neighbors.

"That's good," Lao Tzu stated. He smiled at their shocked reactions.

"Why is having competition good?" growled Sun Tzu. "They're the enemy."

"Yes, but sometimes the enemy can be useful," Lao Tzu said easily, watching Sun Tzu shake his head in disbelief. Lao Tzu was enjoying Sun Tzu's frustration. He addressed Hong-meng, "Just as you need to understand your customer so that you can see his needs, you also need to understand your competition. If you understand the competition, you can use it to become a positive force in the market. That's when competition can be good."

Hong-meng and Sun Tzu looked at each other and shrugged. Lao Tzu laughed, and a bamboo strip suddenly appeared in his hand with the character for yin painted on one side and the sign for yang painted on the other. "You immediately assume that the competition is going to be your enemy…someone who is trying to take all of your business."

"But the competition *is* taking my business," replied Hong-meng.

"You must understand that you and your competition are like yin and yang—the eternal conflict. They are opposites, but by being opposites and by being in conflict, they were able to create the world from chaos. They need each other. The conflict generates qi—energy." Looking at Sun Tzu, he continued, "I agree that a strong competitor can be dangerous, just like an enemy. *There is no worse danger than to underestimate your enemy*. But competition can be a positive force." He turned to stare into the nothingness as if looking for a hidden answer. "*If the sovereign and the people do not do harm to each other then each will benefit*."

"How can each benefit?" Hong-meng queried, convinced that he agreed with Sun Tzu. Competition was dangerous. The competition wasn't good.

"Competition can help create and expand the market," Lao Tzu explained. "It creates interest. It helps create a need. Just as the world needed yin and yang to create something out of nothing, you need competition. You need the yang against your yin to help create a market. Strong competition becomes the qi— the energy to build a larger market." Glancing at Sun Tzu, he continued, "You shouldn't underestimate the capabilities of the competition. That could be fatal to your own business. At the same time, it doesn't need to be a win-or-lose situation. There are advantages to having competition. If you aren't totally blinded by the dangers, you can take advantage of them and use them to create a win-win situation."

"So I don't have to worry about the competition?" Hong-meng didn't believe it for a minute.

"Nonsense! You need to worry about the competition," Sun Tzu said emphatically. "*Only someone who lacks strategic planning and slights an enemy will inevitably be captured by others.*"

Ignoring Sun Tzu's outburst, Lao Tzu went on in a calm voice. "Worry? Maybe it's more accurate to say you don't need to be afraid of the competition." Sun Tzu grunted his disagreement. "The competition should not be feared; it should be understood and respected. Who are they? What is their strength? What are their weaknesses? If you let the competition intimidate you, you've already lost." He watched Hong-meng nod, but knew he didn't agree. "If you let them intimidate you, the competition will take all of your business. If you understand them, you can take advantage of the larger market they help create. If you understand where they are weak, that is where you can attack and gain market share. That's your entry point into the market. If you understand where they're strong, you can prepare for it and protect yourself."

Sun Tzu finally began to see Lao Tzu's point. "*The means by which enlightened rulers and sagacious generals moved and conquered others, that their achievements surpassed the masses, was advanced knowledge.*"

"Exactly!" Lao Tzu pointed a crooked finger at Hong-meng. "Knowledge—that's the key to success. Knowledge of your market. Knowledge of your customer. Knowledge of your competition. Do you remember when we talked about intelligence? We said that intelligent people think they've got all the knowledge they need. They don't need anymore. But that isn't really intelligence. Intelligence should be the part of knowledge that creates more knowledge. Intelligence shouldn't become a barrier to new knowledge. *Can you see everything and know everything without using your intelligence?* You think you already know about your competition and you see them only as the enemy. You've become blinded to the different dimensions of competition." Lao Tzu took a deep breath. "If you can use your intelligence to move beyond your existing knowledge, intelligence becomes a valuable tool. Then you will be able to see the good and the bad sides of competition—and how to use the good to protect yourself from the bad. With knowledge, you can *foresee the bad before it happens.* If you understand your competition, you can anticipate what they'll do and you won't be afraid of them. Knowledge is the tool that will take you beyond the fear and help you manage your competitors to build and strengthen your own market position."

"You say that I need to use the 'good' competition and protect myself from the 'bad.' I can understand that I shouldn't be afraid, but I don't really see how I can use the good part to help me," Hong-meng questioned, looking at Sun Tzu for help. "Even if it's good that they help expand the market, they're still competitors. How can I win business against them?"

"*He who wants to lower someone must first raise him. He who wants to weaken someone must first strengthen him,*" Lao Tzu replied, emphasizing the words *weaken* and *strengthen*. Pointing at the iron tools lying on the ground, he went on, "We've already defined your products, haven't we? If you remember, we said your products were better. Is that correct?" Hong-meng nodded. "We said you had to identify those features that created a product definition that was better than the competition—something that would give you a competitive advantage. We didn't say that your competition made bad products; we just defined yours as being better. We didn't weaken or lower the competition." Lao Tzu picked up the knife. "We don't want to fight the competition by trying to convince the market that they make bad products. Instead, we want to convince the market that your products are better. They have more real value and provide more benefit to the customer. Instead of trying to *lower* the competition, you can use the competition to drive you to produce higher quality products. *The man of worth is the master of men who haven't found the worth.*"

Sun Tzu added, "A man of worth will see and understand the value of his own strengths. *It is sufficient for you to muster your own strength, analyze the enemy, and take them.* You shouldn't underestimate your enemy, but you shouldn't overestimate them, either. Understand what the strengths of the competition are, and also understand your own strengths."

"The competition is not perfect," Lao Tzu said quietly. "They have strengths and weaknesses. *He who stands on the points of his toes will not stay long up. He who takes long steps will not go far.* Look beyond your existing knowledge—your preconceptions—to understand your real competition. You may be surprised at what you find. *The court is well kept, but the fields are full of weeds and the silos are empty.* If you understand your competitors, they won't intimidate you. You won't overreact and you will find your path into the market. You will be able to make decisions based on knowledge rather than fear."

Hong-meng scratched his head, obviously unsure. "I can see that competition can be good because it helps to expand the market. It helps create new interest and new customers. I think I understand that now," he said, although he would have preferred not to have any competition—even good competition.

"There's still another part of competition that is good," Lao Tzu said. "The competition can drive you to deliver quality products, and they will also create an environment where you need to innovate." He handed the knife to Hong-meng. "Remember when we talked about the market being dynamic and how static products quickly die? It's innovation that will create the dynamic products that you need to survive and grow. It's the competition that creates a dynamic market. Competitors become the catalyst to drive your innovation."

Hong-meng was finally beginning to see some of the answers he had been looking for. Competition was good. It created a larger market. It created a demand for quality and drove innovation. But with each answer, he seemed to find new questions. "What about bad competition? Do I have to worry about that?"

Lao Tzu thought for a moment before he replied, "Actually, they're the same competitor. There isn't really a difference." Hong-meng shook his head. How could something be both good and bad? "All competition is good because it helps create and expand your market. Good competition will force you to create high quality products, to offer good service, and to look how you can innovate. It also attracts new customers." He paused for a moment. "Bad competition? Maybe that was the wrong word to use. If we called them dangerous, it might make more sense. All competition is good, and, at the same time, all competition is dangerous. Does that make more sense?" he asked. Hong-meng nodded. "Good. But now I'm probably going to confuse you again. There are really two types of dangerous competitors." Hong-meng stopped nodding, confused again. "I would really call one of the two types bad competition since they don't care about quality or service. They usually don't last long, but they can cause a lot of problems in the market."

"Yes," Sun Tzu agreed. "They're like an army with pretty uniforms who spend all their time in the barracks. They don't really offer any value. *When their wealth is exhausted, they will be extremely hard-pressed.*" His expression showed his disgust. "The normal market competition won't motivate this type of competitor to provide higher quality products or good service. They don't care about having a product definition. The only advantage they offer is price. Because of their poor quality products and poor service, they probably won't get repeat business from customers." He leaned back, taking a deep breath, trying to relax before he continued. "But they do have a good side as well. They attract new customers—they just don't keep them for long. Their weaknesses are easy to find. They never win customer loyalty. They never have repeat customers and they never reach the stage of having happy promoter customers. Their satisfied customers quickly become dissatisfied. Your product quality, value, and service are your weapons against this type of competitor." After a pause, he added, "Even this bad customer can be good. They've created new customers—expanded the market. These dis-satisified customers now become potential new customers for you."

Lao Tzu smiled at Sun Tzu's emotional description of bad competition. "This is also where your product definition becomes very important. This type of competitor will use price to win market share. They will erode the current pricing structure. If your product definition can show real value, you can counter this and maintain your prices. If not, you will be caught in a destructive price war." His smile disappeared. "The second type is the one you really don't want to underestimate."

"Why not?" Hong-meng asked suspiciously.

"Because they're just like you," Sun Tzu answered. "They're proud of their products and they want to build customer loyalty. They won't lose a customer easily. They'll use your weaknesses to win the customer. And when you've established a position in the market, they'll give you no peace. They'll keep trying to take it away from you." He thought about what he'd said for a moment. "Yes, dangerous is definitely a better way to describe them."

"Okay, so I don't want to underestimate my dangerous competition. And I don't want to overestimate them either. What do I do?"

Sun Tzu sat quietly for moment, then pointed to the iron tools. "You want to have competition because it forces you to have better products and helps create a bigger market. But you can only be stronger than your competition if you have clear objectives—if you know where you're going and what you want to accomplish. You need a plan of action."

"What kind of plan?" Hong-meng asked.

"For example: *if they are substantial, prepare for them. If they are strong, avoid them,*" Sun Tzu answered.

"What do you mean?"

"*There is terrain for which one does not contend,*" Sun Tzu stated. "If you really understand your competition, you'll see that they have strengths that you can't beat. Remember, *the army values being victorious; it does not value prolonged warfare.*"

Hong-meng nodded. "So I should avoid those competitors who have a strong position in the market and instead focus my efforts on competitors who show a weakness."

"Right." Sun Tzu was pleased with Hong-meng's progress. "*One who knows when he can fight and when he cannot fight, will be victorious.* If you understand your competition, you'll know if you should attack or not. There are also times when defence will be the best strategy. The competition will not wait for you to do something. You should avoid attacking a strong competitor, but you shouldn't ignore them. That could be fatal. Remember, the competition has their own plans, and those plans will be to find your weak areas and attack you. You need to be prepared to defend your success against attacks from your existing competition—and also from new competition."

"New competition?" Hong-meng asked. That was a depressing thought. He already had enough competition – he didn't need anymore.

"Of course," Lao Tzu answered. "A successful, growing market is always going to attract new competition—good and bad. Not only do you have to understand who your current competition is, you also have to anticipate where new threats to your business are going to come from."

Sun Tzu could see that Hong-meng was having trouble putting it all together. "It's not as confusing as it might sound," he said, trying to reassure him. "You have existing competitors who have strengths, but they also have weaknesses. New competition will be the same. You should attack where they are weak and avoid where they are strong. You also need to create a strong defensive position by setting up barriers."

Lao Tzu interrupted. "Creating barriers is probably the most effective way of stopping potential new competitors. If you've moved your customers to the promoter stage, and your product definition is strong enough, then the barriers to entry for new competition will be so high they will fail before they even start. This is why innovation is so important. Innovation creates new barriers so that the competition is always faced with new obstacles." He could see that Hong-meng liked the idea. "Once you create good barriers, the potential competitor will never become a real competitor. That's why your product definition—along with innovation and understanding your customer—is so important. They're the best barriers you could have for protecting yourself against the competition."

"Attack, avoid, defend," Hong-meng said, trying to summarize what he'd heard. "How do I do this?" he asked more as a plea for help than a question. Avoiding the strengths seemed obvious. But how could he take advantage of his competitors' weaknesses? And how could he defend against new competition that he didn't even know about yet?

Lao Tzu chuckled at the helpless expression on Hong-meng's face. "*A man of worth should be resolute without the use of force.*"

"How can I beat the competition without using force?" Hong-meng looked to Sun Tzu for the answer.

"You don't attack the competition—at least not directly. *A true conqueror doesn't engage in war.* You don't want a total war. *When two equal armies confront each other, the one who hates war will win.*" Seeing Lao Tzu nodding in agreement, Sun Tzu continued, "Nobody wins in a war of competition. A direct confrontation with your competition would be a waste of time and resources. Winning without having to fight is the real objective. *Subjugating the enemy's army without fighting is the true pinnacle of excellence.*"

"How do I beat my competition without confronting them?" Hong-meng was trying to connect the ideas into something that made sense. "How do I fight the competition without fighting?"

"Know your competition and plan. Know your own strengths and use them where the competition is weak," replied Lao Tzu. "And use the barriers of the market to protect your own market."

"*One who, fully prepared, awaits the unprepared, will be victorious,*" added Sun Tzu. "You need to remember that *war is the art of deception.*"

"I can win by deceiving my competition?"

"You can gain a significant advantage when your competition doesn't know what you're going to do next—an important competitive advantage," Lao Tzu said, picking up the knife and handing it to Hong-meng. "For example, we already talked about this knife being your lead product into the market." Hong-meng nodded, holding the knife and turning it in his hand. "But it was only the starting point," Lao Tzu continued. "We decided the customer would then help you define a family of products."

"If you went around to all of your customers bragging about the family of products you were going to make, you would be directly confronting your competition," Sun Tzu added. "Then it simply becomes a race to see who can build the products first. Instead, if you quietly develop and deliver a special knife to the butcher, and then another special knife to a woodworker or the farmer, the competition won't know where you were going to attack next. Don't broadcast your plans, execute them. Don't forewarn the competition of what you're going to do next. *Thus although you are capable, display incapability to them. When committed to employing your forces, feign inactivity. When your objective is nearby, make it appear as if distant; when far away, create the illusion of being nearby.*"

"You could also work *with* your competition," Lao Tzu said, enjoying the surprise on Hong-meng's face. "Yes, that's what I said, work *with* your competition. Or, more exactly, find an area of common interest so that your competitor becomes a partner. Think about the competitors near your shop. Is there anyone that specializes in just one type of tool? Couldn't you work together as a team? You could offer the market a broader selection of products and give a more complete service to your customers."

Hong-meng immediately thought of Lo Tan-chen at the end of the street. He was a craftsman who specialized in high quality, precision woodworking tools for making furniture and ritual vessels. Many of his customers bought their other tools from Hong-meng's competition. If he worked with him, Lo Tan-chen could help introduce Hong-meng to new customers. Hong-meng was sure that when he grew his own customer base, they could also become new potential customers for Lo Tan-chen. Even though there were areas where they would compete, there were even more areas where they could help each other grow. He liked the idea. "*A man of worth should be resolute without the use of force,*" Hong-meng repeated. "So instead of force, I could use deception. I attack the market from different directions, using my new products to keep the competition guessing where I will be next. And I find competitors who can become partners."

Before Sun Tzu could say anything, Lao Tzu spoke up. "*Resolute without pride, exaggeration or ostentation.* Don't let the fog of pride or exaggeration distort what you think your strengths are. And don't let it hide your weaknesses. Deceive the competition, but don't deceive yourself. *He who conquers others is strong. He who conquers himself has the strength of the soul.*"

"Resolute, but not timid. The competition isn't perfect. They'll make mistakes," Sun Tzu said. "*If the enemy opens the door, you must race in.*"

Lao Tzu smiled in agreement. "Exactly. Don't underestimate your own capabilities. You are only limited by your imagination. The competition is an important part of the market—they generate the qi to create an even stronger market. As long as you don't fear the competition; then creativity, innovation, and imagination become your tools to manage that qi and drive your own success. *He who doesn't know his limits can own the kingdom.*"

"I don't want to own the kingdom," Hong-meng said. "I just want to sell my product. And I want to be better than the competition. You told me that I need a plan. I don't attack market areas where the competition is too strong. I don't attack the competition directly. Instead I use deception. I create barriers to stop new competition and protect my position. Is that what you mean by a plan?"

"Yes and no," Sun Tzu replied. "Before you have a plan, you need to know where you're going. What are your goals? What are your objectives? Are you driving the market with your products or are you responding to market needs? What actions are needed?"

"In other words, that is our next question: What's your strategy?" Lao Tzu said.

CHAPTER

7

THE STRATEGY

> Attack a difficulty at its easy points
> Accomplish great works with small acts
> The most difficult thing in the world
> Will reduce itself to the most basic elements.
>
> —LAO TZU

"I thought we had a strategy," Hong-meng countered. "I promote the benefits and strengths of my product to win business from the competition. I don't directly attack my competitors' products, but instead I convince the market that my products are better. I let the competition help to develop and expand the market, and I attack the market where the competition is the weakest. Isn't that a strategy?"

"Is it?" asked Lao Tzu. "Or are those objectives and tactics?" He could see Sun Tzu smiling. Tactics and strategy were something he was an expert in, but instead of interrupting, he kept silent. Lao Tzu continued, "Have you already forgotten that you can't have an answer until you know what the question is? Isn't that what we decided? That you have to start at the beginning? It seems you're making the same mistake again. You're trying to start at the end. You must start at the beginning where the goal is. You can't have a strategy until you know what your goal is—and you can't have objectives until you know what your strategy is. You can't have tactics until you know what your objectives are. You're already working on your tactics before you know where you want to go."

"That's right," Sun Tzu cut in. "The best equipped, most professional army can never be victorious if the soldiers don't know what their goal is. The general who understands the importance of having a clear goal will always have an advantage over those who are unprepared. *One who, fully prepared, awaits the unprepared will be victorious.* Only when the general has a clear goal can he define a strategy. When his officers know what the strategy is, they can define the objectives, and only then can they decide on the tactics."

"Having tactics before you have a goal is like having an answer before you know what the question is," Lao Tzu said, trying to keep the disappointment out of his voice. He had hoped that by now Hong-meng would have understood that he needed to start at the beginning. He shrugged, accepting that people will always look for the easy path and ignore the obvious if they can. "Trying to find a strategy to manage something as dynamic and chaotic as the market when you don't even know what your goal is will lead you nowhere. The goal is your vision of where you want to go, and the strategy tells you how to get there. The objectives tell you where 'there' is, and tactics are what you do."

Sun Tzu smiled at Lao Tzu's description, adding, "The customers, the market, the competition, and your product—each of them needs to be part of your strategy, but they need to be tied together with a common goal. A goal will give you direction; only then can you have a consistent and focused strategy." He followed Lao Tzu's gaze into the distant nothingness. "It's too easy to be distracted by the objectives and tactics and lose track of what your real goal is." As an afterthought, he added, "You want to be successful, don't you? If you don't know what your goal is, how will you know if you've succeeded? If you don't have something to measure yourself against, you are creating motion without any direction."

Lao Tzu could see that Hong-meng was thinking about what he'd heard, but he was sure Hong-meng hadn't completely understood the importance of Sun Tzu's last statement. "To have an effective strategy, you must have a goal that will give you direction. The goal needs to include something that can be measured, or you won't know if you've succeeded."

Hong-meng stared into the nothingness, trying to see the goal and strategy that the others saw. Finally he gave up and asked, "What's the difference between a goal and strategy? Aren't they just different ways of saying the same thing?"

"They are very similar," replied Lao Tzu, smiling as if he'd heard the question a hundred times before. "In fact, if you define your goal correctly, then defining your strategy is very easy. Didn't we decide that your problem is the beginning—the first step—and that we needed to start at the beginning?" Hong-meng agreed. "What you didn't know is that the goal is hidden in the first step. Do you remember what the problem is?"

"I need to find customers who want to buy my product," Hong-meng replied confidently.

"Yes, but didn't we also agree that you have to sell your products for a profit? If I remember correctly, you said you have a family to support. So selling your products for a profit is an important part of your goal."

"It's only 'part of my goal'? Is there more?"

"Yes," replied Lao Tzu. "We've agreed that we want to sell your products for a profit. Is that enough? There should also be something we can aim for that will tell us if we've been successful or not. Do you want to be a major supplier in your market? Or are you happy just having minimum sales every year?"

"I want to be the best," Hong-meng said flatly, as if it were a stupid question to ask.

"Of course," Lao Tzu replied. "That means we need to add something to the goal that says you want to be a major supplier. If we combine the two requirements and move them to a higher level, we are really saying that you want to be a significant, profitable supplier in the tools market. Is that correct?" Hong-meng nodded. "Then that sounds like the right goal. And it's the beginning to defining your strategy."

"To make a strategy from your goal, you need more," Sun Tzu chimed in. "A goal will tell you where you want to go. It can be a high-level statement—maybe even a little abstract. But as soon as you get to the strategy, you need to be precise. That's the real difference between a goal and a strategy. A goal is at a higher level. It's a vision of what you want."

"The goal is like the Tao. *The Tao itself does not act but all is made by it*. It is the vision that creates the strategy," Lao Tzu said in a voice so low that it seemed he was talking to himself.

"The strategy is at the working level," Sun Tzu continued. "It turns the vision into reality. For example, remember we said that for a goal to become a strategy, it has to be measurable. The word *significant* will work as part of the goal because it's a vision of what we want to be, but it needs to be more precise when we define it as a strategy. How many tools can you build in a year?"

"About twenty," Hong-meng answered. Almost as an excuse, he added, "Each tool requires a lot of work to make sure there are no defects."

"Of course. And how many customers do you have today?

Hong-meng looked embarrassed. "I've sold knives to three customers and one ax head." He paused, and then held up four fingers. "I have four customers."

"So as part of our strategy we can make our goal measurable by adding that we want to sell ten tools or increase your number of customers to ten," Sun Tzu said. "This makes our goal measurable."

"Why not more?" asked Hong-meng.

Lao Tzu laughed. "Your ambition is admirable, but you need to be realistic. The third part of an effective strategy is that it must be credible. To have a strategy that is not reachable would defeat the purpose. It becomes a dream and not a strategy."

Hong-meng thought for a moment. "So an effective strategy needs to have a clear direction that supports a goal, it needs to be measurable, and it needs to be credible. Does that mean I have a strategy now? I want to sell my products for a profit to ten new customers." He sat back, smiling, hoping he was closer to being able to go home.

Sun Tzu shook his head, but he was smiling. "No, not yet, but we're getting close." The smile disappeared from Hong-meng's face. It was beginning to look as though he would never make it home. "You must set a time limit," Sun Tzu said. "Without a deadline, your strategy will go on forever. That makes no sense. Not only does it have to be measurable, it also has to be accomplished within a certain time period. If you want to find ten new customers before the end of next winter, then your strategy will support your goal."

Hong-meng asked hopefully, "Does that mean I have a strategy now?"

Lao Tzu shook his head. "We're very close, but there's one more term in the goal that needs more precision."

"Profitability," Hong-meng suggested before Lao Tzu could finish. He was beginning to see how this worked. "We need to define what we mean by profitable. So if we say that I want to sell my products at a price that is twice my cost to ten new customers before the end of next winter, then we have a strategy!"

"Yes," Sun Tzu replied, pleased to see a look triumph and obvious relief on Hong-meng's face. Before he could relax, though, Sun Tzu continued, "You have a clear direction that is measurable and credible with a deadline. But now you have to do it. Having a strategy is not enough if you don't have a plan to execute it. For that, you need to know what your objectives are."

Lao Tzu spoke up. "Remember when we talked about taking small steps to find the right questions so that we can find the right answers?" Hong-meng nodded. "These small steps are the objectives to accomplishing your strategy. Together, they should help reach your goal. *The most difficult thing in the world will reduce itself to the most basic elements.* These basic elements are your objectives— they're the tools you will use to define your tactics. But if you don't have a goal and a clear strategy to define your objectives, your tactics will just be useless motion."

"So I just need to find ten customers and sell them each a tool," Hong-meng stated. "Those are my objectives, aren't they?"

"No." Sun Tzu shook his head. "I'm afraid it's not that simple. You're going to have lots of objectives that will help you reach your goal, and all of these objectives will need to support your strategy. They'll probably change over time as the market develops and new competitors enter. The biggest mistake you can make is to think that an objective becomes a fixed process that never changes. *Thus a large enemy that acts inflexibly will become the captive of the smaller enemy.* So even when you've defined your objectives, you have to make sure that it supports your strategy. If it doesn't, you have to decide if you have the wrong objective, or perhaps you'll have to modify your strategy to align with the market. You must be flexible enough to review your strategy to see if it needs to be modified when the market changes. Don't forget that the market is qi—it is energy, and it's always changing."

Hong-meng said sarcastically, "Now I have to find new strategies every time my objectives change, and keep finding new strategies to keep up with a changing market. I'm not going to have any time to make my products, find customers, or sell my product."

Both Lao Tzu and Sun Tzu laughed at the sarcasm in his voice, which made Hong-meng even angrier. He didn't see anything funny about what he'd said.

"Don't look so depressed, Hong-meng. And don't get mad," Lao Tzu said, trying to keep the laughter out of his voice. "The goal is like the Tao—it is the combination of everything. *The Tao is to the universe like the river beds and valleys are to the river as it goes to the sea.* The goal will guide to where you want to go—just like the Tao. Once you've accepted the Tao, then everything else exists. Once you understand what your goal is, everything begins to fall into place. If you have a clear goal and remember the four elements of a good strategy, the strategy will almost define itself. Then you can focus on the objectives. You still need to remember that the market is made of qi—it's dynamic. *The supreme perfection seems imperfect, his action never stops.* In a dynamic market, there is no such thing as the perfect strategy. It is always imperfect. The action never stops. The objectives are not only your tools to define your tactics, they're also the tools that you can use to test your strategy to make sure it's still in line with the market's needs."

"Objectives are almost like spies," Sun Tzu said. "If they're good, they'll help you define unbeatable tactics. But they'll also be able to tell you when the situation has changed so that you can modify your strategy and still meet your goal. *Thus enlightened rulers and sagacious generals who are able to get intelligent spies will invariably attain great achievements.*"

Sun Tzu grew quiet as he watched Hong-meng organize everything he had heard into something he could understand. Finally breaking the silence, Sun Tzu raised his hand as if to get their attention and said, "We've tried to put everything into nice little categories—a goal, a strategy, objectives—but the world doesn't always fit into simple boxes. It's not that easy." Hong-meng began to ask a question, but Sun Tzu interrupted him. "When you start defining your objectives, you'll find that they have a lot of similarities to your strategy. In fact, a lot of people make the mistake of thinking the objectives are really their strategy."

Hong-meng was not getting any happier with the explanation. "Does that mean that an objective is only a strategy in disguise?" he asked without bothering to hide the sarcasm in his voice.

"In a way, that's correct," Sun Tzu replied, amused at Hong-meng's simplification. "When you're at the strategy level and are defining your objectives, an objective is an objective. Objectives are the small steps you need to take to accomplish your strategy. When you move to the objective level and start defining tactics, that's when the objective works like a strategy. It follows the same rules you used when you defined your strategy." Noting the confusion on Hong-meng's face, he quickly added, "Maybe an example will help explain what I mean. One of the objectives to accomplish our strategy is a strong product definition. We already decided that our product definition was to provide a product that made our customer more productive and that met his needs. Isn't that correct? It wasn't just a list of features." Hong-meng nodded. "But now we have to turn this objective into a tactic or something that we need to do—the action. The objective and the product definition can now be viewed as a product strategy. We can now decide what tactics we need. This product strategy follows the same rules we used for our main strategy. For example, the tactic could be that we want to focus on building a family of iron tools that includes knives, ax heads, and ploughs. This is our direction. Then we want to have minimum of three of each to introduce into the market as lead products. This is something measurable. Based on the market response to the lead products, we will prioritize what other tools we need with a credible plan so that we're not overextending our commitments. And we want to have the tools manufactured within six months—a deadline that meets the requirements of our main strategy."

Hong-meng was beginning to look much happier. Lao Tzu took the chance to interrupt. "If you think about it, we've already defined several of the objectives."

"We have?" Hong-meng replied, scratching his head. "Maybe I don't understand what an objective is."

"That's simple," replied Lao Tzu. He seemed embarrassed. "In fact, we probably broke our own rule of not starting at the beginning, since we talked about some possible objectives before we knew what our goal was and before we had defined our strategy—or at least we talked about where you can find the objectives."

Hong-meng thought back, trying to identify what the objectives were.

"We didn't talk about the objectives directly," Sun Tzu said. "Instead we described where they could be found—in the chaos of the market, in the complexity of the customer, in the value of the product, and the yin and yang of the competition. Objectives could be things like a family of products or a key market segment that needs your products, or even creating barriers against the competition."

"When we talked about the chaos of the market, we said we needed to give it form and order," Hong-meng said thoughtfully. "Within this chaos, we said my market was not the whole market, but only certain segments, and that every person was not a customer." He looked up at Sun Tzu. "So my objective is to focus on a segment of the market where there are customers that need my plough tip." Sun Tzu nodded, encouraging him to continue. "My tactics are then to talk to the farmers who have land north of town, since the ground there is hard and rocky and always breaking their bronze tools. That is the direction. There are nine farmers there, so that is my measurable part. Since there are only nine farmers and there is a definite need for better tools, the tactic is credible and I can do it in less than thirty days, which is my deadline." He was smiling by the time he finished and both Sun Tzu and Lao Tzu were nodding proudly.

"Because you now understand your market and the needs of your customer, you automatically see the objectives without even realizing it," Sun Tzu said. "Now that you understand what an objective is, you'll be able pull them out of your newfound knowledge and use them to create your tactics."

They'd been sitting there for hours, and Sun Tzu had grown stiff from the lack of activity. He stretched his legs, trying to get more comfortable. "You can do the same to define your tactics for the competition. Remember, we said that *one who excels at warfare first establishes himself in a position where he cannot be defeated while not losing any opportunity to defeat the enemy.* One of your objectives will be to identify and attack the weaknesses of your competitors. Another objective will be to defend your own market position by creating barriers. Your tactics will include what you need to do to expand your market as well as what you need to do to defend your existing market position.

Hong-meng thought back to what they'd said. "Also with respect to the market," he added, "we said we needed to focus on market segments that *need* my product and don't just *want* it. So, as I said earlier, my objectives are to identify market segments where there is a need for my products and then define tactics that will use my product to build a path into the market."

"Exactly!" Lao Tzu exclaimed. "If you go back over our conversation, you'll see that we've already found several objectives that would support our strategy. But we've still forgotten one very important thing about objectives and tactics! We didn't ask ourselves if they will help us meet our goal. Do they support our strategy?" He paused, and a small tree branch suddenly appeared in his hand. A spider was busily building a web between two small stems on the branch. "Your objectives are like the strands of this web. Each strand has its own strength and purpose, but the real strength happens when all the strands work together, combined into one strong, solid design. The web is your strategy, and the objectives are the strands. When they are aligned so that they support each other, they create a strong web—a strong strategy." The branch disappeared from Lao Tzu's hand. "It's too easy to get lost in the excitement of your objectives and tactics and forget that they need to support your goal and strategy. Just having objectives and tactics is not good enough. They need to work together. Otherwise, we have a lot of motion and no action."

"What do you mean?" Hong-meng asked.

This time Sun Tzu was the first to answer. "Motion and action—don't confuse the two. Action is productive. It contributes to reaching a goal. Motion is unproductive—it accomplishes nothing except making it look as though you're busy."

"Right," Lao Tzu chimed in. "When you have objectives and tactics that follow your strategy and are focused on reaching your goal, then that's action. You also need to test your tactics to make sure they really support your strategy and meet your goal. If they don't, you're just using up energy for nothing. That's motion."

"Are the tactics you defined for the market motion or action? Will they help you reach your goal to sell products at a profit?" Lao Tzu asked. "You need to ask yourself these questions to confirm that your tactics, objectives, strategy, and goal are aligned. Since the market is dynamic, it's always changing, and it's easy to react to these changes with new tactics and forget about your strategy and goal."

"What about your tactics to enter the market?" Sun Tzu asked. "Do they follow your strategy and still meet your goal?"

Hong-meng thought about it for a moment. "I think so. We decided to focus only on those segments that need my product and not waste time and effort chasing everything. That would be my objective. The tactic is to select one segment where my product will create the path to the customer who needs it. They are both in line with my goal to be significant, as well as with my strategy to sell to ten new customers."

Lao Tzu nodded. "What about your product? Are the tactics in line with your goal?"

"Yes," replied Hong-meng confidently. "*One fashions the clay to make a vase, but it's the emptiness inside that makes it useful.* We defined the product so that the customer could see that it was better than the competition. We understood where the real value was. We identified the emptiness of the product. We created value that the customer will pay for. That meets are goal of being profitable. And the need creates the path into the market for new customers, supporting significance."

"We also decided how to create a family of products to give you an even stronger position in the market and to confuse the competition," Lao Tzu added. "*Create disorder in their forces and take them.*"

"Exactly," replied Hong-meng. "Having a stronger position in the market is again in line with being significant and increasing the number of customers I have."

Hong-meng fell silent, thinking about what they'd discussed. The others patiently waited for him to continue. Finally he said, "The objective for the customer seems to be more difficult." He stroked his beard, searching for the words to continue. "The customer is hidden in the fog of chaos—the market. We decided that attracting the customer by showing him some profit was better than chasing every shadow. *Display profits to entice them.* That's a more productive use of our time, so I guess that could be one objective. I need to look for a tactic that will pull the customer out of the fog, but I also need an objective that will move my customers through the various stages from suspicious to promoter. For the customer, it seems that I need several objectives. Is that correct?" He looked hopefully at Sun Tzu and Lao Tzu.

"That's right," Sun Tzu responded. "You need to understand your customers—understand what they need and what will win their interest. So you're right. We already said that the customer is multidimensional and very complex, and that's why you'll probably need to look for several objectives that will help meet your goal. " He paused for a moment. "The same is true for the competition. If you understand the competition, you'll know how you can win business and reach your goal. *Do not intercept well-ordered flags, do not attack well-regulated formations.* Take advantage of their weaknesses and your strengths."

"Understand and respect your competition, but don't fear them," Lao Tzu said. "Many people make the mistake of being so focused on their fear of the competition that their strategy is driven by this fear. The competition drives the definition of their strategy instead of just being one part of it."

Sun Tzu agreed, "Don't let the competition define your strategy. Your strategy should make you unconquerable. *Thus one who excels in warfare is able to make himself unconquerable.*"

"It's true that if we let the competition define our strategy, we'll create a weak, one-dimensional strategy that will get in the way of our being a significant tool supplier in the market," Lao Tzu said. "But we also need to determine whether our strategy is market-driven or product-driven." Before Hong-meng could ask the obvious question, Lao Tzu continued, "You've already shown that you're very proud of your iron tools. This pride could influence you to define your strategy around your products instead of focusing on the market's needs. Your strategy should be driven by what your customers need and not on your own pride for your product."

After a respectful pause, Sun Tzu broke the silence. "Our objectives and strategy seem to be in line with reaching the goal that we want, but we've forgotten something very important."

"What?" Hong-meng asked.

"We've found our goal and defined a strategy that will support that goal," Sun Tzu stated. "We also understand what objectives are and how they will be used to create tactics. We understand our customers and the competition, and we know how to define a product. But we still haven't found this magical path into the market that our product is supposed to build for us."

"Yes," Lao Tzu said slowly. "We need to find those objectives that will overcome the barriers to enter the market. Our next question is: what objectives can help us build a path into the market?"

CHAPTER

8

VALUE

> **The goodness is like the water which favorises everyone and is rivalled by nothing.**
>
> —Lao Tzu

How long had he been on Kunlun Mountain? Time had no meaning here, but Hong-meng knew he'd been there too long. He was tired and wanted to go home. He sat in the nothingness and watched the shadows drift across the horizon. Shadows! There shouldn't be shadows in the nothingness. He blinked, trying to focus. Yes, he could see shadows! He was beginning to see something! Sun Tzu and Lao Tzu watched him carefully.

"What is the value of your product?" Lao Tzu asked, breaking the silence and bringing Hong-meng's thoughts back to the summit of the mountain.

"Value of my product? What do you mean?" he answered, still not believing there could be shadows in the nothingness.

"We said that part of your goal was to sell your product at a profit. Is that right?" Lao Tzu asked. "Pricing is one of the objectives that will create that profit, and at the same time it can open a path into the market. In order to create a pricing strategy so that you can define your tactics, you must determine what value your product has. If your price is too high, you will create a barrier. If your price is too low, you won't meet your goal of being profitable. Does your product have enough value to make a profit?"

Hong-meng wasn't sure how to answer. He'd never really thought about the value of his product before. He knew what it cost him to make, and he just added a *peng* or two to the cost. "I don't know," he finally said. "I don't know what the value is. I know what the cost is. Is that what you mean?"

Sun Tzu shook his head. "Let me guess—you simply add a *peng* or two to your cost and that's what you try and sell it for. Am I right?" Hong-meng nodded, not sure if he should be embarrassed. Sun Tzu went on in a slightly sarcastic tone, "I'm sure you don't even know what the customer is willing to pay. Do you know what the competition sells their products for?"

This time Hong-meng was really ashamed. "Not always." He hesitated, and then added, "I never asked."

Now Lao Tzu was shaking his head. "Knowledge. I thought we agreed that knowledge was important."

"Your product is better than the bronze tools your competition sells," Sun Tzu said. "Is that what you said?" Hong-meng nodded. "If better is important, then better should have a value, shouldn't it?" The question seemed rhetorical, so Hong-meng didn't bother to answer.

"And you also said that your iron tools will last longer than bronze tools. They don't break as easily and they're easier to repair." Hong-meng was still nodding. It was safer than saying something. "If that's correct, then it should be easy for you to define the value of your product."

Sun Tzu was convinced that Hong-meng didn't understand what they were talking about. He reached over and picked up the iron plough tip and began to speak as if he were instructing a group of students. "The farmer is using a bronze plough tip today that's old and has been repaired many times. He needs a new one. You want him to buy your iron plough tip. You know he needs a new plough tip, so you've found the need. You create interest by telling him that your plough tip will make him more productive, since it will stay sharper longer and when it hits a stone, it won't be damaged. He sees the value. You have need and interest. Now what do you sell the iron plough tip for?"

Hong-meng thought for a minute and replied, "Seventeen *peng*."

"Why?" Lao Tzu asked, leading Hong-meng to the answer he already knew.

"Simple. My cost is fifteen *peng* and I add two for my profit."

"And what does your competition sell their bronze plough tips for?" asked Lao Tzu.

"About the same. Or maybe only sixteen *peng*."

"So maybe you can get one *peng* more for having a better product?" Lao Tzu suggested, enjoying the trap that Hong-meng was walking into. Hong-meng nodded.

Sun Tzu couldn't hide his sarcasm. "Don't you think your product has any real value?" He raised his hand to stop the objection from Hong-meng. "Or maybe it's simply that you don't understand the real value," he said, handing the plough tip to Hong-meng. He let him inspect the tool for a moment before he continued, "The bronze plough tip will need to be replaced every two years. Your iron tool will last at least five to six years—almost three times longer. The value of your product should be at least two to three times that of the bronze tool. In addition, you could ask the customer how many times he has to get it repaired and how much time he loses. Lost time also adds value to your tool."

"So I could charge the customer at least fifty *peng*?" Hong-meng was surprised that he hadn't thought of that himself.

Lao Tzu shook his head and explained, "Not necessarily. You can prove that fifty *peng* is the real value of your product compared to the competition's bronze tools. But what is it worth to the customer?" Hong-meng didn't know. *Weren't value and worth the same thing?* he wondered.

Sun Tzu continued, seeing that Hong-meng's thoughts were finally drifting in the direction of the answers. "That's why we said you need to understand your market and your customers," he said without sarcasm. "A rich farmer will see the value and might be willing to pay something close to fifty *peng*. A poor farmer whose total salary for the year is only fifty *peng* might also see the value, but it's not worth it to him to pay one year's salary for the tool. He would prefer to pay only sixteen *peng* for the bronze tool, or maybe twenty *peng* for the increased value of your tool."

"Having a clear and well-defined pricing objective is a key part to reaching your profitability goal. It can also be a valuable tool in finding new customers and gaining entry into new markets. Pricing is one of those objectives that will build your path into the market. Cost, value, worth, and profitability are the four key elements needed to create an effective pricing strategy," Lao Tzu added.

"They can only be successful if you know how to use them and if you know your market and your customers," corrected Sun Tzu, seeing Lao Tzu nod in agreement. "If your customers are all poor farmers, then your pricing strategy can't be fifty *peng*. You need to understand what they're willing to pay."

Hong-meng thought about it for a few moments. "My market includes both poor and rich farmers. Does that mean I should have two different prices?"

Lao Tzu laughed. "Life isn't that simple. We already talked about the answer to that. We said you need a family of products."

Sun Tzu chimed in, "*The unorthodox and orthodox mutually produce each other, just like an endless cycle.*"

Lao Tzu grinned at Sun Tzu's interruption and took the plough tip from Hong-meng. He held it up so that the sun reflected off the metal. "The unorthodox might be the answer," he said simply. "For example, you already said you can only make twenty tools a year. Higher quality requires more work. What do you do with the tools that don't meet your quality standards—ones that might have a small defect?"

"I either rework them, which means more effort, or I melt them down and start again," Hong-meng replied.

"Even if the defect doesn't affect the functionality of the tool?" Sun Tzu asked.

"Of course!" replied Hong-meng, insulted that someone would ask the question.

"You want to succeed, don't you?" Sun Tzu asked in a harsher tone. "You must open your mind and start looking for value where you don't think value exists. Value can wear different faces. You just need to know how to look for it."

"What Sun Tzu means is that a tool with a defect that doesn't affect its functionality still has some value," Lao Tzu explained. "Instead of reworking them or melting them down, you could offer them to poor farmers at a price they can afford. The higher quality tools will still be stamped with the Hong-meng character and sold at a higher price, but the other tools don't need to be rejected. If the defects don't affect functionality, the tools can be used to address another market segment—the poor farmer."

"Yes, that's what I meant," Sun Tzu agreed. "By seeing value where you hadn't seen it before, you can increase your productivity and increase your potential market size. The branding used for the high quality tools will create a strong market position for you, and at the same time give you very good profitability.

The tools with small defects will bring you new customers that you normally wouldn't be able to get at the higher price."

Hong-meng liked the strategy. He reached over and picked up the knife. "And I can do the same with all of my tools?"

"Yes," replied Sun Tzu. "But only if you understand the cost and the value of your product as well as its worth to your customers and your market. Having a good pricing strategy is one of the key objectives in making sure you reach your goal of profitability. It can also be used very effectively to find and create a path into the market."

Sun Tzu became unusually quiet, obviously thinking through an idea and how he should present it. Finally he grabbed the ax head and said, "But that's not all. Sometimes a pricing strategy can be more unorthodox."

"What do you mean?" Hong-meng asked.

"*The wise must contemplate the intermixture of gain and loss,*" he replied simply. "When we were talking about the market, we said we needed to find a path into it where you could establish a strong position. Pricing strategy can help you do that. It can help promote your tools."

Lao Tzu understood what Sun Tzu was saying and he continued the idea. "There will probably be key market segments that you want to be in, but you need to get past the first obstacle, where the customer starts using your product." He could see that Hong-meng wasn't following. "Remember how we talked about obstacles to entering the market? One of those obstacles is distrust. Another is disinterest, or maybe it's a competitor who is already established. The potential customer doesn't trust your claims that your product is better and isn't interested in changing. He likes the tools he's been getting from your competitor." Pointing at the ax head, he asked, "What's the cost of that tool?"

"About ten *peng*."

"For a key customer, you could use your pricing strategy as a way to beat the obstacles and get him to start using your iron tools," Lao Tzu stated. "Use it as a key to open doors to new customers. You could sell it for only five *peng*, or maybe even give it away for free so that he'll start using your tools and find out for himself the real benefits—and value." He paused and, before Hong-meng could reply, added, "If your claims are really true about the benefits of your products, he'll come back and buy other tools from you at the real price, where you can make a profit."

"This supports part of your strategy—to increase the number of customers," Sun Tzu said. "We talked about the objectives being the strands of the web. Well, the web is only strong if all of the strands work together. This is a good example of using one strand, pricing, to add strength to another strand, promotion. Each one in isolation doesn't make sense, since they seem to break the rule that all objectives need to support our strategy. It's only when they work together that they build a stronger web. Together, they support our strategy and help break down the obstacles so that we can build a path into the market."

"After you've built your path, your next objective is to transform this unprofitable satisfied customer into a profitable repeat customer," Lao Tzu explained. "That's when you reach the other part of your strategy—profitability."

Hong-meng wasn't convinced that giving away his tools for free was a good strategy, but he had to admit there had been several customers in the past for whom it might've helped overcome their resistance. He didn't like it, but he felt it was worth thinking about if it would help win new customers.

"Pricing strategy is an important objective," Sun Tzu continued, interrupting Hong-meng's thoughts. "Not only for reaching your goal of profitability, but also to support your other objectives. But you must be careful and always make sure that your pricing strategy will ultimately help you reach your goal. *If it is not advantageous, do not move.* If you are too aggressive with your pricing strategy, you might get more customers. but you're no longer reaching your goal of profitability."

"That's true," Lao Tzu agreed. "You'd have a huge share of the market, but no profit. But there might be other ways to expand where profitability doesn't need to be sacrificed to get new customers."

CHAPTER

9

SOMETHING IN THE NOTHING

> **Walk well, is to walk without leaving a trail or trace. Speak well, is to speak without committing errors or incurring reproaches. The man of worth is the master of men who hasn't found the worth.**
>
> —LAO TZU

"I think he's talking about promoting your products," Sun Tzu clarified. "That's probably the next objective we need to look at for building your path into the market."

Lao Tzu rose from his kneeling position and slowly paced the area. He was lost in his own thoughts, staring into the nothingness. The nothingness had changed, though. Hong-meng could see more shadows in it, almost as if something was trying to escape from it. Lao Tzu shook his head as if he couldn't find the answers to his own questions and returned to the present. In a quiet voice he asked, "How should you promote your products? Is that the question we want to ask?" Hong-meng was listening, but he wasn't sure that the question was directed at him. Since he didn't know what the answer was, he decided to stay silent.

Shrugging, Lao Tzu sat back down. "*By beautiful words, one can buy the honors.*"

Since Lao Tzu was looking directly at him, Hong-meng felt he needed to say something. "Beautiful words… Why do I need beautiful words?" He held up the ax head and added, "The customer only needs to try my product to know its better."

"I agree," Sun Tzu said with a puzzled expression. "Beautiful words are just going to get in the way."

"I thought we were going to answer the question of how to promote my products," Hong-meng said. "Are you saying we need beautiful words?"

Lao Tzu was enjoying the game he was playing. "When you go into the market in Qufu, are you overwhelmed by vendors trying to sell you their products? How do you select which merchant to buy from? The ones who find the right words to get your attention?"

"Maybe," Hong-meng answered cautiously. He thought back to his small shop. He could hear vendors shouting out their messages, trying to get attention from the people milling about between the various stands and booths. Individual messages quickly became lost in the noise of hundreds of messages. Success seemed to be driven by whoever could shout the loudest, or whoever could outlast the others. Occasionally someone was able to attract attention from potential customers with a unique message. "But I don't really believe what they're saying. They might sound beautiful, but I want proof that the product is good."

"*True words are not agreeable. Agreeable words are not true.* Is that what you mean? The truth is not really eloquent, and eloquent words make you distrustful," Lao Tzu replied. "*The supreme eloquence appears to stammer.*"

Sun Tzu was becoming frustrated with the direction of the conversation. "What's the purpose of promotion?" Pointing an accusing finger at Lao Tzu, he went on, "You seem to be saying that promotion is simply standing in the market, shouting out the benefits of your product or maybe exaggerating the features just to attract a possible customer."

"What's the purpose of promotion?" repeated Lao Tzu, stroking his beard slowly. A triumphant smile played on his lips. "Thank you, Sun Tzu. That's the real question we want to answer. How to promote your products is irrelevant for now. It's one of those questions that get in the way of the really important questions. What's the *purpose* of promotion? First we need to know what we want to accomplish, then we can decide how to do it." Raising an eyebrow, he asked, "Is the purpose to promote the benefits of the product, or is it to attract new customers?"

"Both," growled Sun Tzu, unhappy that he'd been used by Lao Tzu to present his ideas.

"Can't we do that in the market?" Lao Tzu asked Hong-meng.

Without thinking, Hong-meng replied, "It wouldn't do any good. The customers in the market are there to buy vegetables. They're not shopping for tools."

"I see," Lao Tzu replied, still playing his game. "They're not your customers and it's not your market. Is that what you're trying to say?"

"Okay, now I understand what you're trying to do with your silly game," Sun Tzu piped in, his anger beginning to disappear. "A promotion strategy must be designed to address the real customer and the real market for the product. You need to know who your target audience is, or you'll just have motion again and not action."

"*By beautiful words, one can buy the honours,*" Lao Tzu repeated. "But the beautiful words will have a different purpose in our market. They need to create things like brand awareness and visibility in the market without exaggerating the benefits and the features of the iron tools. The words need to be the *profit* that pulls the customers out of the fog." To emphasize his point he picked up the ax head. "*He who doesn't glorify himself and his merit, will be recognized. He who brags will not shine.*" He paused to give the other two time to think about what he'd said. "We're back to your question about the purpose of promotion. Is it to brag or glorify, or does it have another purpose?"

"You said it is to create brand awareness and visibility in the market," Hong-meng replied. "But I don't understand how that will help me sell more tools."

Before Lao Tzu could say anything, Sun Tzu interrupted, "I already explained that. We're back to action versus motion. We must determine who our customer is, where the market is, and what the customer needs so that we can define a successful promotion strategy. The words must address the needs of the customer—show him the profit and not *glorify* the product. Even more important, we need to know what we want to accomplish, or we will just have motion. Yelling out the benefits of your product in the marketplace is motion. We want to use promotion to create effective brand awareness, highlight your product definition, and find a strong position in the market—that's action. Make sure your message focuses on the needs of the customer and is not simply bragging about the features of your products. It should be aligned with your other objectives or you'll create objectives that are not focused on reaching your goal."

"If you've defined your message correctly, then promotion can be a valuable tool to support your other objectives," Lao Tzu added. "For example, the competition helped create a larger market for us, and we can obviously use promotion to take advantage of that, but it needs to be aligned with our other objectives, as well. Don't forget about the spiderweb. We already showed how you can use pricing to support your promotion strategy. The same is true for promotion. It can be used to support your other objectives, such as product definition, market expansion, competition, and barriers, so that the web becomes even stronger. Promotion becomes a critical objective for a successful strategy. If we really have a better product with a large potential market and we keep it secret, that's disastrous. It's almost criminal." He paused for a moment and then asked, "Have we defined what the purpose of our promotion is?"

"To support our strategy and objectives," Sun Tzu replied, nodding.

"Yes!" Lao Tzu exclaimed. The wrinkles on his face melted into a smile as he addressed Hong-meng. "The main reason we need promotion is to give additional support to our other objectives and our strategy. The competition helped to expand the market. We need promotion to make us visible in this larger market and to attract more customers. Our product has significant advantages that will benefit the customer, but we still need to tell the market that. Promotion will help deliver that message. Now all we need to do is look back over our other objectives and define what kind of promotion strategies we need to support them." He could see that Hong-meng followed his train of thought. "We don't want to do promotion just to do promotion. That's motion. We want a promotion strategy that will help us reach our goal. That's action. Promotion alone won't be able to do that, but when you use it to support your other objectives, then everything becomes aligned to reach your goal and support your strategy."

Hong-meng was smiling, but he wasn't really sure why. "How do I use this idea of promotion?"

"That might be easier than you think," Lao Tzu said. "We already talked about one way. Use your existing customers. You already have an objective to move your customer from suspicious to promoter. When you've done that, you've already accomplished one promotion objective. Promotion is used to deliver a message. You just need to go back through the objectives we already set and ask yourself what the key message of the objective is."

"Key message?" Hong-meng repeated.

"Of course," Lao Tzu said. "For example, you don't promote the features of your product. Instead you use the product definition for your promotion so that you highlight how it meets the needs of the customer. Promotion can only be effective if the message is relevant to the customer. When we talked about competition, we decided to focus on areas where the competition was weak and you were strong. Your message should focus on your strengths in these specific market segments. You also have key messages about the real value of your product. All these messages can and should be turned into promotion."

Hong-meng folded his hands in his lap. He was almost embarrassed. "How do I turn these messages into promotion?"

"There's no easy answer to that," Lao Tzu replied seriously. "Creativity is one part of it. One of the most valuable uses of creativity is to be able to turn your objectives and messages around so that they are communicated to the market from the perspective of the customer's needs. Don't use the messages to glorify your products. Use them to reinforce how they benefit the customer. Remember that when you defined your product, you redefined the features so that the value met the needs of the customer. It was no longer just a list of features. You need to do the same with the messages. The customer should hear how it benefits them."

"I'm sure the market in Qufu is like any other market," Sun Tzu continued. "It's very noisy, with every vendor shouting out the features of his products. Successful vendors are those that can break through that noise with something special—a strong, unique message that attracts the attention of the potential customer. That something special is a message that focuses on creating the customer need so that they move beyond want."

Hong-meng thought about it for a moment. "Okay. If I can find these creative messages that I can use to promote my products and get a strong position in the market, how do I deliver the messages? Do I need to go to every city and stand in the market shouting out my message?"

"That's a good question," Lao Tzu commented. "But I think the question we really need to answer is what channels you can use to deliver your key message and your products."

Hong-meng couldn't believe his eyes. Suddenly he had noticed that the shadows in the nothingness had grown into valleys with cliffs and treelined ridges that disappeared in the distance. The nothingness had become something. Sun Tzu and Lao Tzu were also watching the scenery, but they didn't seem surprised.

Lao Tzu broke the silence by asking, "Do you remember Zhuang Zhou?"

Hong-meng answered, "Yes. He said I should listen with my mind."

"Exactly." Lao Tzu laughed. "He has another saying about man's place in the world. *The world is vast and immense, but man can only use the part under his foot.*"

Hong-meng smiled in understanding. "What you're trying to tell me is that my market is *vast* and that I'm just one person trying to attack it. Is that correct?"

Lao Tzu nodded. "The need for your product is not going to be limited to the city of Qufu, or even to the province of Lu. There will be a market for your products in Song, Wei, Qi, and Chu Provinces, as well." He pointed a crooked finger at Hong-meng. "If you want to succeed and stay competitive, you must always look for ways to expand your business, but if you try to cover your whole market, you'll quickly run out of time and energy. And you'll probably fail. *If the spirit does not become efficient it will self-destruct.*"

Hong-meng replied cautiously, "If I promote my tools properly in Qufu, the benefits they offer will spread by word of mouth. Customers will come to me to buy tools. Isn't that true? I don't need to cover the whole market."

Sun Tzu shook his head angrily. "You can't trust word of mouth to spread the message. And besides, how will you deliver your products to all your new customers in Wei or Qi? Word of mouth can't do that! Your new customers aren't going to wait months for their tools."

Lao Tzu nodded his agreement. "All the other strategies and objectives we talked about are going to be wasted if you don't have a plan to communicate and work directly with your new customers. What you need is a…"

"…an objective," Sun Tzu finished. "You need an objective that defines channels to new markets and customers."

"Okay, I need another objective." Hong-meng's irritation was beginning to show again. "What is a channel?" He looked from Sun Tzu to Lao Tzu.

"That's probably not the right question," Lao Tzu replied gently, trying to avoid being too blunt. "Or at least it's not the first question. You probably should be asking what the purpose of a channel is. When you know what it should do, then defining what it is will be a lot easier."

Hong-meng was embarrassed at being corrected. "Okay. Then what is the purpose of a channel?"

"We've already answered that!" Sun Tzu said impatiently. "The channels will be used to deliver your message and product to your markets and customers." Lao Tzu started to interrupt, but decided against it and sat back quietly.

Hong-meng's embarrassment was changing to frustration and anger. "Well, if I already know the answer to the first question, can I now ask the second question? What is a channel?"

Sun Tzu answered in a quieter voice, "A channel is like an army attacking a position. Just like an army, you must understand the terrain, your objectives, and your enemy. You also need to focus on your strengths. *If we are concentrated into a single force while he is fragmented into ten, then we attack him with ten times his strength.*"

"Let's not forget about your goal, strategy, and the other objectives," Lao Tzu interrupted.

"Exactly," Sun Tzu agreed. "Your channel strategy needs to be in line with your other objectives and it needs to support your strategy. Having channels into markets where the competition is strong is a waste of time and resources. *One who cannot be victorious assumes a defensive position; one who can be victorious attacks.* Your focus should be consistent with the objectives we decided on for beating the competition. Focus on their weaknesses. Focus on the terrain where they aren't in control. *Thus the strategic configuration of power of those that excel in warfare is sharply focused, their constraints are precise.*"

Lao Tzu could see Hong-meng's uncertainty. "Let's make it simple. Let's go back to the first question—the purpose of the channel. A channel is used for promotion and delivery of your product. It needs to support and agree with your other objectives—otherwise, it makes no contribution to reaching your goal. It should be installed to support markets where you're strong and your competition is weak. It must target customers that need your product, where promoting the benefits will be effective. It shouldn't chase customers that don't need your product. It should promote the value of your product and convince the customers of its worth." He took a deep breath. "In short, the channels are your path into the market, and they work together with your other objectives to reach your goal."

"As I already said, it's like an army," Sun Tzu stated again, trying to stay with a subject that he understood. "An army needs to understand the enemy—its strengths and weaknesses. But an army also needs to understand its own strengths and weaknesses. It needs to understand the terrain and how to use it. Then it needs to have a plan—a strategy and objectives. Finally, it needs to execute it—the tactics."

"I'm not an army," Hong-meng protested. "I'm only one person. I can *only use the part under his foot.*" He tried not to sound too depressed.

"That's why you need an army," Sun Tzu said stubbornly.

"I don't have an army. Besides, I'm not a general. I have no idea how to run an army." He no longer bothered trying to hide his frustration.

"The army is already there. You just have to find them and use them," Lao Tzu replied with a smile. "Your existing customers are one channel that we talked about. Finding a competitor you can work with as a partner is another type of channel. Merchants travel between the different provinces. It would be easy for you to convince them to carry your products with them for a little extra money. There are also merchants in the other provinces that already sell bronze tools. If your tools are really good and can be easily sold, they'd be happy to sell your tools for you—for a percentage of the profits."

"Isn't that against our goal?"

"No. In fact, it shows how important the goal is," replied Lao Tzu. "Before, you only thought about your manufacturing costs. That's always a dangerous trap to fall into. You're so focused on the development of your products that you never see the other costs. There will always be additional costs to implement your tactics. That's why understanding the value and worth of your product is so important. You need to make enough profit so that you can invest part of it to implement all of your tactics. Otherwise, you'll never reach your goal."

"I still don't know how to run an army." Hong-meng looked at Sun Tzu.

Sun Tzu thought about how he should reply without confusing Hong-meng even more. Finally, he said, "*In general, commanding a large number is like commanding a few. It is a question of dividing up the numbers. Fighting with a large number is like fighting with a few. It is a question of configuration and designation.* Configuration and designation are the key points. They will support your objectives of focusing only on those customers who need your products in markets where you're stronger than the competition."

"What are configuration and designation?" Lao Tzu asked, anticipating Hong-meng's next question. "They mean that you want your channels to be an extension of you. For example, if you've done a good job in educating and training them, you've successfully configured and designated and you won't have to spend all your time supervising them. That's always the danger with channels into the market. You can become so focused on them that you forget about the customers."

Sun Tzu nodded his agreement and said, "Don't forget that the market is chaos and the customer is emotional and always changing his mind. Your channels need to be flexible to adapt to the changes. *One who is able to change and transform in accord with the enemy and wrest victory is termed spiritual.* And don't forget about the competition. The more successful you are, the more they'll try to attack you from all directions. *In military combat what is most difficult is turning the circuitous into the straight, turning adversity into advantage.*" Sun Tzu sat back.

"Hopefully you can see now that you need to have good channels to implement your strategy," Lao Tzu said. "The purpose of a channel isn't that complicated, but you need to be careful. People drive these channels, and since they're people, they'll only be effective if they can trust you and know that they'll be successful with you. They need to understand your strategy as much as you do."

"*On whose orders are consistently carried out has established a mutual relationship with people,*" added Sun Tzu. "You must have a relationship with them so that they'll have the same goal as you. They literally become an extension of you. They're your eyes, ears, and arms into the bigger market."

"Which, if you think about it, is the solution to the problem we talked about earlier, that *man can only use the part under his foot,*" Lao Tzu explained. "If you've selected good channels that know the market and the customers and understand the real value of your products, it will almost be like you've multiplied yourself into all these new markets. They'll be able to promote the benefits of your tools and provide a service so that you'll have happy customers."

Sun Tzu sighed in relief. He'd become impatient and was looking for an excuse to leave. "Finally! Since you now have happy customers in an expanded market, it's a good time for me to say good-bye." He stood slowly and bowed formally to the other two. Lao Tzu nodded in return, while Hong-meng bowed, showing his respect for the famous military strategist. Sun Tzu disappeared down the trail leading into the something that had arisen from the nothingness.

Lao Tzu smiled as he watched Sun Tzu disappear into the distant landscape. A stubborn man, he thought, but one who is worthy of his reputation. *Walk well, is to walk without leaving a trail or trace. Speak well, is to speak without committing errors or incurring reproaches.*

He reached over and picked up his large straw hat, placing it on his head before he rose to his feet, using his walking stick for balance. Looking back at Hong-meng, he said in a quiet voice, "You've learned your lessons well, Hong-meng. You can now see the something in the nothing." He waved his hand across the nothingness that was now something. "I've no doubt that you'll succeed in your ambitions. Today was only the beginning. Knowledge is like the Tao. *The Tao is like a vase that usage can never fill. It is like an abyss, the origin of everything.* What you've learned here is the beginning that has no end. It's like my colleague Lie

Zi once said, '*The end and the beginning are things that begin without end. The beginning of the one is the end of the other, the end of one is the beginning of the other.*'" With that, Lao Tzu turned and followed a different trail down the slope of Kunlun Mountain, disappearing into the something that had arisen from nothing.

Hong-meng was tired, but it was a good tired. It was time to go home. He looked across the valley from his position on the summit of the magical mountain. He was happy. He could see something in the nothing.

REFERENCES

Tao-tö king, Lao-tseu, Traduit par Liou Kia-hway, Editions Gallimard, 1967

Les Trente-Six Strategèmes, Traduit et commenté par Francois Kircher, Editions
    Payot & Rivages, 1995

Le Taoïsme, Martin Palmer, Editions Payot & Rivages, 1997

Comprendre le Tao, Isabelle Robinet, Editions Albin Michel, 2002

Lao Zi et le Tao, Isabelle Robinet, Bayrd Editions, 1996

Histoire de la Pensée Chinoise, Anne Cheng, Editions du Seuil, 1997

Art of War, Sun Tzu, translated and commentary by Ralph D. Sawyer, Westview
    Press, 1994

China, A New History, John King Fairbank, Belknap Press of Harvard Univ.
    Press, 1992

Histoire de la Chine, René Grousset, Editions Payot & Rivages, 1994

www.ingramcontent.com/pod-product-compliance
Lightning Source LLC
Chambersburg PA
CBHW051342170526
45166CB00002B/919